CHILD ALIVE

Child Alive

New insights into the
development of young children

Edited by ROGER LEWIN

TEMPLE SMITH • LONDON

40695

First published in Great Britain 1975
by Maurice Temple Smith Ltd
37 Great Russell Street, London WC1
This book is based on a series of articles
first published in the magazine
New Scientist during 1974
© 1974, 1975 IPC Magazines Ltd
ISBN 0 8511 7072 2
Printed in Great Britain by
Clarke, Doble & Brendon Ltd
Plymouth

Contents

Preface   7

Introduction

1   The birth of human developmental psychology   9
    MICHAEL RUTTER

Interactions between Mother and Infant

2   The first hours, and the smile   14
    AIDAN MACFARLANE

3   Early separation   23
    MARTIN RICHARDS

4   Social development in infancy   32
    RUDOLPH SCHAFFER

5   Are mothers stimulating?   40
    ANTHONY COSTELLO

Children at Play

6   The importance of play   50
    JEROME BRUNER

Language

7   Early attempts at speech   62
    COLWYN TREVARTHEN

8   Speech makes babies move   81
    WILLIAM CONDON

9   The development of language   91
    JOANNA RYAN

10 Acquisition of grammar   98
    RICHARD CROMER

Cognitive Development

11 Competent newborns   112
    TOM BOWER
12 Mother's face and the newborn   126
    GENEVIEVE CARPENTER
13 The growth of skill   137
    KEVIN CONNOLLY
14 Children's inferences   149
    PETER BRYANT

Sex Differences in Behaviour

15 Sex differences: biology and behaviour   158
    CORINNE HUTT
16 Sex differences: biological and social interaction   167
    JOHN ARCHER AND BARBARA LLOYD

Development of the Brain

17 Nutrition and brain growth   180
    ROGER LEWIN
18 Brain development and the environment   193
    ROGER LEWIN

Conclusion

19 A child's life   208
    MICHAEL RUTTER

Bibliography   220

Notes on the authors   227

Preface

The human infant is now at the centre of one of the most exciting and rapidly expanding areas of current psychological research: developmental psychology. Recent years have seen an accelerating number of researchers beginning to study the way newborn infants perceive their world, the way they make use of apparently innate models of the physical relationships within their environment, and above all the extraordinarily high learning capacity of very young babies.

The combined efforts of the hundreds of developmental psychologists now probing the first weeks and months of human life are generating a torrent of knowledge about the abilities—innate and learnt—of young infants and a stream of new ideas about what it all means. Inevitably, there are disagreements on the interpretation of results; the discoveries and views presented by the authors in this book demonstrate this to some extent. But such differences reflect research in ferment, in a state of intense excitement and productivity. All the researchers agree on one thing, however: that the newborn human infant has been grossly underestimated, and we are now beginning to learn just how wrong the old ideas were.

I am indebted to Dr Peter Bryant, Professor Kevin Connolly and Dr Martin Richards for their help and guidance in producing an overview of the fruitful and important area of research presented in this book.

ROGER LEWIN

The birth of human developmental psychology

MICHAEL RUTTER

Up to about the turn of the century children were mainly regarded as just little adults. But recent research demonstrates that compared with the notions of even a few years ago, infants are more variable and individualistic; they are more active in their influence on the environment; and the processes by which they learn as they develop social relationships are not what they were thought to be. The burgeoning science of developmental psychology is only just beginning to show what it can achieve, but already the results are causing a rethinking in terms of ideas on child development, on education and learning and on the early influences which lead to mental disorder.

The rapid period of growth in child psychology was initiated by the work of Stanley Hall, James Sully and others just before the turn of the century. The impetus came from several directions. The development of psychoanalysis opened people's eyes to the richness of children's thinking and to the importance of the early years for later development. It was characteristic of the times, however, that Freud's account of infantile sexuality was based entirely on the memories of adults, unaided by any direct observations of children. Following Alfred Binet, there came the large-scale development of intelligence testing and about the same time services for delinquent and emotionally disturbed children began to be established. In Britain, with his astonishing range of high quality psychometric investigation, the late Sir Cyril Burt did more than anyone else to make child psychology a respected field of study.

During the 1920s and 1930s naturalistic studies of young children first came into their own with the work of A. T. Jersild, Florence Goodenough and F. B. Holmes. Although not widely known in the English-speaking world until later, this was the time Jean Piaget commenced his pioneering studies of children's learning. A whole series of long-term longitudinal studies were established in the United States, and a little later Arnold Gesell and his followers began their careful charting of children's growth and development. The work of John Watson and the behaviourists also stimulated an interest in environmental influences on development.

In spite of its manifest theoretical and practical importance, child psychology went into an unexpected decline in the 1940s. People became disenchanted with the long-term longitudinal studies which seemed to lack point and focus and naturalistic studies faded out. Experimental psychology became the high prestige area and young children did not seem to be suitable subjects for this sort of research. Research on parenthood continued, but this too lost popularity as the deficiencies of the interview as a means of obtaining retrospective information became only too clear. There were pleas for more direct study of children, but the studies which were undertaken came under severe methodological criticisms. Theories of personality, of educational practice, and of mental disorders continued to place great emphasis on early psychological development but the theories remained static for a lack of new questions and a lack of fresh data. Predictive psychological studies seemed to have reached their limit and there was a growing unrest with the notions of measuring fixed intellectual capacity.

Just over two decades ago, several things happened which provided the necessary fillip to research in this area and which eventually led to the major advances in developmental psychology now taking place. Piaget's emphasis on the dynamic *process* of learning, as distinct from *levels* of knowledge or intellectual capacity, transformed cognitive psychology. At first, the effect was to produce a dreary series of repetitive replications of his observations and an uncritical acceptance of his theories as a basis for teaching young children. But then researchers began to challenge the dogma and question the psychological mechanisms he proposed. The result was the growth of a variety of novel and ingenious studies of young children's learning and cognitive performance.

John Bowlby's 1951 report for the World Health Organisation on the effects of maternal deprivation not only led to a remarkable change in outlook concerning residential services for children but also stimulated a wealth of research on early child development. His claims regarding the devastating effects of early deprivation were met with serious criticism concerning the weakness of his evidence. The criticisms were justified and some of his claims have since been found to be wrong in detail. Nevertheless his views provided a much needed focus for research.

Three years earlier Donald Hebb had published his classic *The Organisation of Behaviour* in which he outlined his ideas on the importance of experience in the development of intelligence. This had as revolutionary an impact in the field of animal studies and later on developmental psychology as Bowlby's work did on the world of child care. At the same time, B. F. Skinner's concepts of development in terms of responses to rewards and punishments led to an upsurge of research into operant conditioning of young children. Partly as a reaction against what some regarded as epidemic environmentalism, there was a renewal of interest in individual differences. Unlike the earlier genetic view of an inevitable unfolding of development, individual differences were now thought of as influencing interactions with the environment and studies of parent-child interaction received a new focus.

These theoretical issues provided a vast range of developmental questions requiring an answer. However, progress might have been slow were it not for advances in technology. Perhaps the single most important advance was the realisation that quite simple motor responses (limb and head movements, for example) could be used to gauge complex perceptual discriminations. Infants' ability to distinguish between different visual or auditory stimuli could be assessed provided that the response required was nothing more complicated than turning the head or sucking. Operant conditioning (conditioning of behaviour in terms of the response it elicits) came into its own as an invaluable tool in teaching babies to make these simple responses as a means of studying perceptual development.

Once psychologists realised that infants could be studied, there was a flurry of research activity which soon led to a variety of sophisticated investigative techniques. The other advance was the spread to human psychology of some of the methods used in studying animal behaviour. Although some of the theoretical tenets of ethology (learning about human behaviour by studying animals' behaviour) have been discredited, the marriage between the observational skills it brought and the quantification methods deriving from psychology proved very fruitful in leading to a rebirth of naturalistic studies of young children.

INTERACTIONS
BETWEEN MOTHER AND INFANT

The long-held idea that very young infants lead a relatively passive existence means that until recently psychologists have more or less ignored the newborn and early period. But new research shows this to have been a mistake.

Even brief separation of mother and child immediately after birth can have lasting effects on the relationship between them. The development of social interaction—through touching, breast feeding, and eye-to-eye contact—begins at birth. The newborn baby displays inbuilt rhythms—in dreaming and sucking behaviour for instance—and these soon expand into direct social contact through visual and vocal signalling. The inbuilt rhythms are a prelude to intentional and deliberate signalling by the baby.

As the child grows the issue of mother/infant interaction moves into the question of how much does the mother influence the infant's development; how important is environmental stimulation; is the upbringing of children in small families significantly· different from that in large families; and how special is the life of a twin?

(Incidentally, throughout this book the term 'mother' has been used for convenience. It does not imply that there is anything special or obligatory in the adult involved being the mother. Rather it refers to the person, or persons, most concerned with rearing the infant.)

The first hours, and the smile
AIDAN MACFARLANE

Infants did not develop in order to be attractive to their care-takers, nor did caretakers develop simply to be good at looking after infants. The interaction between parent and child has developed as a single system, allowing great variation.

The factors affecting early interaction between mother and child are numerous. To try to define lines of causality between external influences and proposed consequences is very difficult and complicated. For example, work by Arnold Sameroff and his colleagues at Rochester University, USA, shows a relationship between psychiatric problems during pregnancy and difficulties during delivery. Helena Kraemer and her colleagues at Stanford University have shown associations between length of labour and neonatal behaviour, and Yvonne Brackbill and Martin Richards have shown an association between medication during labour and neonatal behaviour. Martin Richards and Judy Bernal at Cambridge have also shown that neonatal behaviour influences the mother's behaviour. On the other hand, one could also hypothesise that mothers who are anxious during pregnancy may also be anxious after delivery and that this will alter the way they look after their infant and thus alter the infant's behaviour—and that they may independently receive more medication during labour.

First encounter between mother and infant
In Oxford, as in many other centres, we are attempting to untangle some of these problems, and one of the studies we are doing is looking at the way mothers greet their babies immediately after delivery in the labour room, and seeing if this correlates in any way with behaviour later on. The study is not yet complete, but videotapes of the initial contact between mothers and their babies do in part confirm the findings of Marshall Klaus in Cleveland that mothers 'tend to go through

an orderly and predictable pattern of behaviour' beginning with finger-tip touching, caressing and manipulating the limbs. In many cases, however, this represents only a very small part of the total behaviour as shown by the transcript of one delivery. It can be seen how the mother verbalises her inspection of her child—involves the father—imitates the child and puts her own interpretation on the child's behaviour. From these initial tapes we also noted how much maternal behaviour seemed to be influenced by the type of delivery, the medication used, whether the father was present or not, and how well the mother knew her medical attendants. Marshall Klaus's films were taken between thirty minutes and twelve hours after birth with the infant naked under a radiant heater, whereas our tapes were taken in the labour room within five or ten minutes of birth, with the child partially covered.

In order to see how neonatal behaviour may interact with maternal behaviour, we have included in the same study a Neonatal Behavioural Assessment Scale which has been developed by an American paediatrician, Berry Brazelton, working at Boston Children's Hospital, USA. This consists of 27 behaviourally defined items each scored on a nine-point scale, such as alertness, irritability, and lability of state. The critical behaviour patterns for these can be elicited by a trained observer using only a bell, a brightly coloured ball, a rattle and a torch as supplementary apparatus. If one adds the abilities which can be shown using more complicated apparatus— visual preferences for flashing rather than still lights, for contour, for certain brightnesses, for the human face and more specifically the eyes, auditory preference for high-pitched sounds, ability to appreciate three-dimensional objects—one soon learns not only what a remarkable range of performance the neonate has, but also how much individual variation there is between them. even immediately after birth. Unlike Tom Bower (see Chapter 11), I do not believe that psychological processes begin at birth, but rather that they begin at conception, and that in the womb the child is subjected to a large number of stimuli—such as chemical, kinesthetic, and auditory,

Transcript of a mother in immediate post-delivery period

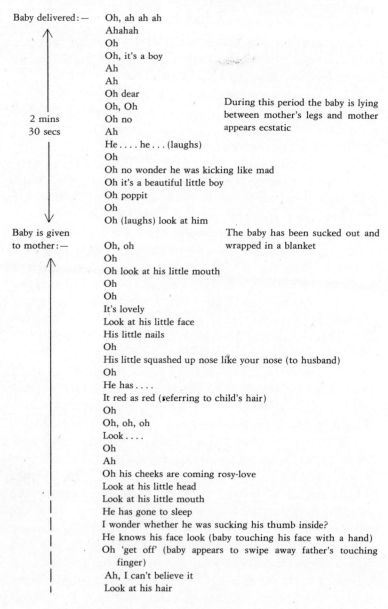

Baby delivered:—

↑

2 mins
30 secs

↓

Oh, ah ah ah
Ahahah
Oh
Oh, it's a boy
Ah
Ah
Oh dear
Oh, Oh
Oh no
Ah
He . . . . he . . . (laughs)
Oh
Oh no wonder he was kicking like mad
Oh it's a beautiful little boy
Oh poppit
Oh
Oh (laughs) look at him

During this period the baby is lying between mother's legs and mother appears ecstatic

Baby is given
to mother:—

↑

Oh, oh
Oh
Oh look at his little mouth
Oh
Oh
It's lovely
Look at his little face
His little nails
Oh
His little squashed up nose like your nose (to husband)
Oh
He has . . . .
It red as red (referring to child's hair)
Oh
Oh, oh, oh
Look . . . .
Oh
Ah
Oh his cheeks are coming rosy-love
Look at his little head
Look at his little mouth
He has gone to sleep
I wonder whether he was sucking his thumb inside?
He knows his face look (baby touching his face with a hand)
Oh 'get off' (baby appears to swipe away father's touching finger)
Ah, I can't believe it
Look at his hair

The baby has been sucked out and wrapped in a blanket

Oh look it's all fair there

He is going a nice colour now, aren't you (to baby)

He's sucking his thumb

How anyone can anyone feel sick at it, I don't know (mother referring to people feeling sick when present at birth)

Oh you poppit

It wasn't bad

He was, wasn't he?

Oh dear what did you do that for? (to indistinguishable action by baby)

He's blowing bubbles

His little hands are all wrinkled

Looks like he's done the washing doesn't he?

He looks . . . .

No, we knew it was going to be a boy didn't we? (to husband)

That's why it's a boy

11 mins Open your eyes then (to baby)

45 secs Ahh (laughs)

Can you open your eyes then? (to baby)

He's scratched himself by the look of it, on his face

Oh (pain with contraction in third stage of labour)

No he's resting on me

Hello (as baby opens his eyes for first time)

Oh he's going (imitates baby's blinking)

Hello (laughs)

Oh his eyes are all stuck

Hello

Dark blue (referring to eyes)

Hello, look

He's got your eyes (to husband)

Look you've got beautiful blue eyes (to baby)

What are you looking at me like that for? (to baby)

Hello

Oh, he's got a beautiful face

Yah (delivery of placenta)

How long do they usually take to open their eyes?

He's got one open now

We will have to give you a bath in a minute won't we?

Hello

Hello

You can really grip can't you (to baby)

Ah (injection)

Did he seem to hold your finger? (to husband)

Did he?

He wants to open his mouth, look

We will see if we can give him a feed in a minute

Baby given
to father

both from his environment and from his own actions—and that it is the interaction of these interuterine experiences and the infant's genetic make-up that leads to the variation in newborn behaviour.

Much of the newborn child's behaviour will be of more surprise to the psychologist than the mother. To the mother some of these abilities will simply be included in the humanness of her infant. For instance, the one-month-old's ability to appreciate a three-dimensional object might be noticed by the mother as the baby reaching out when a bottle is put to its lips. Mothers are good observers of their infants, though they tend to negate their findings in the face of vicariously acquired information. Thus when I recently tested babies' effective visual field, many of the mothers remarked on their babies' ability to visually follow their face—but then went on to say that of course babies could not see. Some of the information acquired by mothers is from out-of-date psychological work— thus when mothers in another of our studies were questioned as to when they thought that their babies could differentiate between them and a stranger, they replied 'in the first couple of weeks, but of course that's not possible'. Recent work by Louis Sander in America does show that in the first two weeks, neonates respond differently according to whether the care-taker is the usual one or a new one, and Genevieve Carpenter (see Chapter 12) has shown how very young infants responded differently to a stranger's face and voice, than a mother's face and voice.

Along these lines, my colleagues and I at Oxford have recently completed a study to investigate whether babies could recognise their own mother's smell (many mothers having remarked that it was obvious that they could). Using head turning as an indicator of preference I found that at two days of age babies turned the same amount to another mother's breast pad as they did towards their own mother's breast pad. However, by ten days after birth they turned their heads significantly more towards their own mother's breast pad, indicating their ability at this age to discriminate between their own mother and another mother on the basis of smell.

When is the first smile?

The more overt forms of behaviour that caretakers respond to are smiling, crying, eye-to-eye contact, babbling, vomiting, winding, coughing, and dirtying and wetting nappies. On the first of these, Charles Darwin with his own children, observed: 'This infant smiled when 45 days, a second infant when 48 days old; and these were true smiles, indicative of pleasure, for their eyes brightened and eyelids slightly closed. The smiles arose chiefly when looking at their mother, and were therefore probably of mental origin.' Darwin was an accurate observer and it would be interesting to hypothesise that in the last century, social smiling in babies did not in fact occur till nearly eight weeks old. However, more recent studies in the 1960s by D. G. Freedman and Peter Wolff in the USA show that 'endogenous' smiling occurs from birth. Endogenous meant in this case that there did not appear to be any external stimulus giving rise to the smile.

This endogenous smiling has been found by Emde and Harrison to occur about eleven times in every hundred minutes and to be associated with certain arousal states, or changes of state, and with a recognisable electro encephalographic pattern. It probably begins pre-birth and continues till five or six months. Wolff, however, found that smiling could be elicited in the first week of life by a variety of noises, including a high pitched voice. The first clear indication of a social smile appeared during the third week when a human voice became a better elicitor than mechanical noises, and in the fourth week when eye-to-eye contact became an effective elicitor by itself. This observation was further strengthened by the finding that a plain cut out cardboard face with ring and large dots for eyes would at this stage also elicit smiling. Till the fourth week Wolff had the impression that babies tended to focus on the back of the head rather than on the eyes. On the other hand, work by Slater and Finley at Durham on infant eye movements suggests that even when a baby appears to be looking directly at one's eyes, he may in fact be fixating some point adjacent to them.

Tony Ambrose, at the Behavioural Research Unit in London,

has shown that the time of onset of social smiling and the amount of smiling could be varied with the amount of social stimulation, and Yvonne Brackbill at Georgetown, USA, discovered that smiling could be increased or decreased in babies by reinforcement. Studies of premature babies demonstrate that the onset of social smiling is more closely related to age from conception than age from birth, suggesting a maturational factor, and the probable innateness of smiling, by the finding that social smiling occurs in blind and deaf and blind/deaf infants—although later—between ten weeks and six months.

The baby's smile and the mother

But how does this behaviour affect the mother? In another study we asked mothers of two-month-old, first babies, the question 'What sort of thing do you enjoy most about your baby?' Seventy-five per cent of the mothers included in the reply 'Smiling'; yet among a similar group of mothers with babies only one month old, not one mentioned smiling.

Two of the questions which arise from these findings are: (1) If Wolff's findings are correct and babies develop social smiling at three weeks, why have not mothers noticed it till after the end of the fourth week? (2) If social smiling plays such a prominent part in the attractiveness of the child, then why does it not appear till one month of age, rather than at birth, so that the mother would be optimally attracted to her child as early as possible?

The answer to the first question is the simpler. Wolff used a group of highly sophisticated babies whom he had followed from birth and to whom he had given a great deal of stimulation; he was therefore probably duplicating Tony Ambrose's findings that the onset of social smiling can be brought forward by stimulation. Also we have noted—as has Klaus—that within a short time of birth mothers express great interest in their babies' eyes (see the transcript, where the mother first 'greets' her child when he opens his eyes and then goes on to imitate the eye opening episode).

Kenneth Robson and Howard Moss at the Department of Psychiatry, Tufts New England Medical Centre, found in a study of 54 mothers having their first babies, that the feeling of 'strangeness' towards their offspring only ceased when the baby started 'looking as if he recognised objects in his surroundings', and a small number said that eye-to-eye contact released strong positive feelings. Unfortunately it is extremely difficult, when observing mothers with their babies, to tell either when the mother is looking at her baby's eyes or when the baby is looking at hers. In such observations one usually has to say that mother and baby are in the *en face* position, that is, in a position where they can look at one another's faces. Researchers in the department in Oxford are developing an eye movement recorder which operates remotely, requires no attachment to the head, and gives an analogue output of eye position in real time. Using this apparatus it may be possible to look at babies' scanning patterns, especially of their mother's face. Thus, if Wolff's observation that true eye-to-eye contact does not begin till four weeks is right, this might be the feature in social smiling that is of importance to the mother.

Why not smile at birth?

The second question is very much more difficult to answer, for as D. G. Freedman pointed out (for scientists rather than for mothers, though the two are by no means exclusive) 'Behaviour, like the smile or cry, must be considered in terms of total hominid adaptation, including the total life span.' In these terms, the appearance of social smiling at three or four weeks is the result of a large number of evolutionary pressures, including those influencing the maturational state of the brain at birth. I would hypothesise that one evolutionary force might be the very high maternal and infant mortality that existed in our species until recently. If there is—using Dr Christopher Ounsted's term—a period of courtship between mother and baby in which social interaction and communication develop, instead of immediate attachment in the perinatal period, it has the advantages to the child that should his mother die, he can develop an interaction with some other caretaker. The advantage to the mother is that should her infant die shortly after birth, her reaction would be such as neither to prevent her from continuing to function in a manner needed for survival, nor to decrease her chances in participating in producing further children.

Smiling and eye-to-eye contact are forms of behaviour which can be studied in isolation, but in our studies we are attempting to look at them and other behaviours, in terms of the developing interaction and communication between caretaker and infant.

Early separation
MARTIN RICHARDS

Though the issue of mother-child separation is an old one in developmental psychology, it was not brought to the fore until 1951 when John Bowlby formulated his theory of attachment in which he placed great emphasis on the potential damage that might follow maternal separation in the early years of a child's life. This work has had a profound effect on social policy and has become a central theme for all those concerned with child care, particularly in the area of the provision of substitute care for children without families. However, most of this concern, both in terms of theory and social policy, has been related to children of at least six months and older. Much less attention has been paid to separation in the first weeks of life.

New ideas on separation
The lack of interest in early separation is understandable because Bowlby's theory suggested that ill effects for the child occurred when an attachment with the mother was broken. As it was thought that it took several months to build an attachment, separation in the first weeks was not seen to be of any special consequence. However, recent research has modified Bowlby's original theory and the processes involved are now believed to be much more complex than the formation of a bond with the mother. In particular, some of the long-term effects for the child may arise because of changes in the attitudes of the adults caring for him that follow a period of separation. There is no reason why a process like this should only have an influence with older children.

Another reason why separation was not thought to be important for very young infants is that newborns were often assumed to be too immature to be much influenced by their environment, provided, of course, that they received the basic requirements such as food and warmth. But with the growing appreciation of the capabilities of babies (as is described in several of the other chapters in this book) this has seemed less and less reasonable. In this chapter, I will discuss early separation of infants from mothers and its possible long-term consequences. Much of the evidence is incomplete but it does seem to provide a consistent picture which is disquieting in several respects.

Impact of hospital births

In Britain and America more than ninety per cent of all babies are born in hospital. In most hospitals, mothers are separated from their infants for at least brief periods and sometimes the separation is prolonged. The latter is particularly likely if the babies receive special care because of sickness, low birth weight, and so on. For some this will involve a prolonged period in an incubator and the mother will leave the hospital long before her child. At best, contact will be maintained during visits which are frequently brief and widely spaced in spite of growing encouragement for greater contact from doctors. About fourteen per cent of all babies (in Britain) receive some form of special care.

Enormous strides have been made in the physical care of sick and low-birth-weight babies as can be seen from the improvements in the perinatal mortality and morbidity statistics. But as the new patterns of paediatrics have tended to increase separation, the improvements in the statistics may have been achieved at some psychological cost to parents and children. Are there long-term psychological effects of early separation? And what is the evidence?

It might seem a relatively simple matter to set up a study that would be a direct test of the hypothesis that early separation has long-term consequences. However, the difficulties are legion. As mothers are not usually separated from their newborn babies without some reason, it is very difficult to find separation and non-separation groups that are comparable in all other respects. This is particularly true when one is dealing with the low-birth-weight babies that are among those separated for the longest periods. Any investigation must be able to distinguish the possible effects of low birth weight itself and its attendant complications from the influences of separation. Studies have shown that low-birth-weight infants are different from the rest of the population at school age in both intellectual and social behaviour but we cannot conclude that this is the result of early separation.

Studies of early separation

However, direct studies have been carried out in the United States where separation tends to be more extreme than in this country. Marshall Klaus, John Kennel and their colleagues at Cleveland have compared groups of full-term babies under a traditional hospital routine which involved total separation for the first forty-eight hours and then four-hourly reunions for feeding with a 'high contact' group who were together except for very brief periods from birth. In terms of paediatric assessments and mothers' reports of their feelings about their babies, differences were found throughout the first year. Other research has used various methods to increase contact between incubator babies and their mothers. Though the evidence is less clear cut because of methodological problems, there are indications of faster weight gain, better scores in paediatric examinations and ratings indicative of a more satisfactory mother-infant relationship after the decreased separation. Some of these differences have been reported well beyond the neonatal period though no long-term follow-up studies have yet been reported.

The idea of separation does not in itself constitute a psychological theory—it merely describes a particular state of affairs. So the question has to be asked: Why do early episodes of separation influence the later mother-child relationships? Various hypotheses have been put forward. Several American workers have borrowed the concept of a critical or sensitive period from the animal ethologists and have suggested that there is a brief optimal time after delivery during which the mother is able to form an attachment to her baby. If contact is denied during this period, the mother is much less able to form a satisfactory attachment—or so it has been argued. There is no evidence that directly supports this position and the experience of adoptive mothers, who presumably form their relationships outside any sensitive period, does not give any support to the idea.

A factor that has come out of many studies is the mother's self-confidence. The more contact she has, and perhaps even more importantly, the more responsibility she is allowed for the care of her child, the sooner the mother becomes self-confident and assured about her ability to look after the baby. Such a factor might be especially vital after the birth of a low-birth-weight baby because many mothers seem to feel that a premature birth implies a failure on their part to carry a pregnancy successfully, and their confidence is often particularly damaged.

Another way in which separation could influence a mother is by giving her an implicit model of how she should care for her baby. If she does not see her baby for a day or so after delivery and then only at a brief feed each four hours (as is not unusual in American hospitals) the mother may then leave the hospital with the idea that this is the natural and expected pattern of the relationship which she should continue when she gets home. After all the hospital is run by paediatric and obstetric experts so it is reasonable for her to conclude that the pattern of contact laid down there is what modern science has 'proved' to be best. Most mothers could hardly be expected to analyse the situation and conclude, as some social scientists have done, that the hospital routine is a product of the institutional structure and the convenience of doctors and nurses and has very little to do with the interests of either mother or baby.

The factors I have mentioned so far affect the mother. However, if they change her relationship with the baby, it is likely that in turn they will influence the baby's development.

Sensory deprivation in an incubator
A rather different theoretical approach has emphasised the possible direct effects of early experience on the baby. Workers

in this tradition have pointed out that an incubator approaches the sensory deprivation situation for the baby. Physical conditions tend to be constant and unchanging and quite unlike the sensory world provided by the uterus or by a typical maternal pattern of caretaking in the home. Using analogies from experiments with rats which suggest that early sensory stimulation is necessary for healthy development, they have set up intervention programmes for babies in incubators that provide changing visual and auditory stimulation and frequent touching and holding from nurses. Such programmes have resulted in faster weight gain and better results in paediatric assessments. It should be noted that experiments in this theoretical tradition take no note of any special relationship between the mother and the child and they are only concerned with the stimulation received by the baby—from whatever source. However, studies that attempt to increase mother-infant contact may also increase the stimulation received by the baby so there is an area of overlap between the two kinds of studies.

Our approach to the problem has been indirect. We have analysed the growth of the mother-infant relationship in the first few days and tried to relate our results to neonatal events. We have found clear indications of the effects of a 'psychological' separation which can occur even when the mother and infant are in physical proximity. This happens when the infant's condition does not allow it to play a full role in the reciprocal interchanges with the mother. After this psychological separation, changed patterns of mother-infant interaction are set up which may persist for many months, if not longer.

Analgesics during labour

The clearest case of psychological separation occurs when the mothers have received an analgesic drug during labour. In our sample Pethilorfan was often used. This is a mixture of the narcotic Pethidine (meperidine) and the narcotic antagenist Levallorphan which, when given to the mother, passes rapidly through the placenta to the baby. After the administration of Pethilorfan, infants suffer from mild respiratory depression and are slower to breathe and cry at birth (though are still well within a clinically 'normal' range). Throughout the first ten days, in our observations of feeding sessions, we find differences between the drug and non-drug babies. The length of the feeds is shorter after Pethilorfan. This is confirmed by other investigators who have found reduced food intake after obstetric medication. The actual patterns of the feeds provide other differences. The babies are sleepy and unresponsive and the mothers have to work to get them to suck and stay awake. The lengths of the sucking bouts are reduced and mothers intervene more frequently in attempts to get the babies sucking. At later ages differences emerge in observations of social interaction (play) situations. These are rather hard to summarise and our data analysis is not yet complete but, in broad terms, at both thirty and sixty weeks the drug babies are less closely involved in social interchanges with their mothers and show more self-stimulatory activities like thumb sucking.

As yet we cannot be sure that these later differences are the result of changed interaction patterns in the early days rather than the direct consequences of long-term changes in the nervous system brought about by the drugs at birth, but the weight of the evidence seems to point to the former. We have no information about consequences beyond the first year. However, it is unlikely that an event that had led to a different path of development in the first twelve months will not continue to have some influence; though it is, of course, possible that the influence is of no great practical importance. But until this has been demonstrated beyond all doubt, we should be very cautious about dismissing the drug effects as trivial.

Separation and breast feeding

Other evidence of the consequences of psychological and physical separation comes from our studies of lactation. Paediatric opinion has increasingly supported breast feeding in recent years and we were interested in factors that might be associated with its successful establishment. As is already

well known, we found that breast feeding was strongly correlated with a mother's educational background and social
position. Not only were middle class mothers more likely to
begin breast feeding, but they were more successful; success
being measured either by the duration of lactation or whether
a mother breast fed for as long as she initially planned. But
given that many mothers did not manage to feed for as long
as they had hoped to, we wanted to see if we could isolate factors
that were important in determining success or failure. Again
separation was the factor that stood out.

An analysis of diaries kept by mothers during the first ten
days showed that breast feeding mothers fed more frequently
than bottle feeders (breast feeding mean: 6.6 feeds per twenty-
four hours; bottle feeding 6.0). The usual professional advice
offered to the mothers in our sample was that they should aim
at feeding at four-hourly intervals and where possible miss a
feed in the early hours of the morning. If followed exactly this
would give a mean of 5.0 feeds per twenty-four hours—a minimum achieved by only one mother in our sample. Given this,
and that breast feeds are required more frequently than bottle
feeds (breast milk has a lower protein content on a volume-for-
volume basis) it was not surprising to find that the unsuccessful breast feeders were more likely to have expressed rigid
intentions about the scheduling of feeds during a prenatal
interview. Mothers who gave up breast feeding frequently
said they had done so because they did not have enough milk
to satisfy their baby who failed to sleep for three and a half to
four hours and often woke and cried two to three hours after
a feed. Our data indicates that this is the usual pattern at this
stage of lactation. But mothers who gave up the attempt to
breast feed interpreted the two to three hour sleeps as a failure
on their part to provide enough milk rather than a reason to
increase the frequency of feeds. The explanations for the social
class differences in success and failure are complex but part of
it involves the middle-class mothers' tendency to fit their feeding to their babies' needs rather than sticking to the standard
advice.

Crying was found to be more frequent in breast fed infants and there was a difference in the response to crying between those who gave up within two weeks and the more successful breast feeders. Those who continued breast feeding were more likely to respond to a bout of crying with a feed rather than another kind of intervention. This is further evidence of the willingness of successful breast feeders to adapt their routines to the needs of their babies and so reduce separation. In view of this, we were not surprised to find a direct positive correlation between the mean length of crying bouts in the first ten days and the duration of lactation. So, factors that tend to restrict feeding contact in the first ten days are associated with less successful breast feeding.

Comparative evidence confirms this picture. Across a wide range of animal species there is an association between milk composition, infant growth rates and the frequency of mother-offspring contact. In terms of frequency of contact, at one extreme there are species like the rabbit that spend a few minutes per day with their young and at the other, rats or some monkey species where contact is virtually continuous. On this scale, the composition of human milk would put us among the continuous species.

Of course it might be objected that, though all this might be true of lactation, it does not necessarily apply to other aspects of maternal behaviour, and just because lack of contact reduces the probability of successful breast feeding it does not mean that it will have any serious consequences for the child's development. This must be granted. However, lactation is part of the whole complex of mother-infant interaction and, if it is disturbed by separation, it would be wise to suppose the same is true for other aspects of the relationship—at least until we have hard evidence to the contrary.

Further support comes from the consideration of the evolutionary history of mother-child relations. Though we do not have any direct evidence, it is reasonable to argue by analogy from the surviving non-agricultural peoples. In the early weeks, mother-child contact is almost continuous. The baby is carried around on the mother's body and usually sleeps beside her at night. It is not unreasonable to assume that this was the basic pattern throughout the greater proportion of man's evolutionary past. Much has changed fundamentally since the development of agriculture and it would be absurd to think that all the changes are for the worse. But again, the extent of the change and its relatively recent origin should make us pause to consider the situation.

As I said at the beginning, the evidence for ill effects of early separation is incomplete and much of it indirect. If it were visualised as a chain, the chain would have many weak links and a slight tug would be sufficient to break it. But a jigsaw puzzle might be a better analogy for complex questions such as this. The few pieces we have so far do seem to belong to the same jigsaw puzzle and are beginning to fit into place.

Social development in infancy
RUDOLPH SCHAFFER

It is often said that babies do little except feed and sleep. Even if this were true, analysis of these two behaviour patterns alone soon reveals the enormous complexity of psychological functioning present even in the earliest weeks of life. They show that the infant is by no means like a lump of clay that remains formless until it is taken in hand by the baby's parents and shaped according to society's wishes. It seems, on the contrary, that the infant comes into the world already equipped with a particular kind of behavioural organisation which his caretakers must respect and to which they must adapt their own behaviour. The work that has accumulated in recent years on early psychological development has provided us not only with new insights into infant behaviour but has indicated also a radically different picture of the socialisation process compared with that which formerly prevailed.

Sleep as organised behaviour
Let us look at the nature of the infant's innate behaviour by first examining his sleep. It was twenty years ago that Nathan Kleitman and his colleagues at the University of Chicago first established the existence of two distinct phases of sleep, an active phase and a quiescent phase. The distinction was originally based on the observational concurrence of bodily motility and bursts of rapid eye movement (REM) but has since been given even greater substance by the addition of physiological measures such as brain waves, heart rate, and respiration. As, however, the rapid eye movements provide the most notable criterion, the two phases have come to be known mostly as REM sleep and NREM (no-REM) sleep, and as such have been described not only in man but also in a wide range of other species.

These two phases are already present in the infant from

birth onwards. Compared with the adult there are a number of differences, particularly in the nature of some of the brain wave patterns and in the fact that infants invariably begin sleep with a REM phase whereas adults start with NREM sleep. There are other differences too. But the highly regular cyclic alternation of the phases, found even in the newborn, leave no doubt that we are confronted here by an endogenously organised behaviour pattern and that the infant's periods of sleeping and wakefulness are thus regulated by an internal clock of considerable accuracy.

In the adult each REM-NREM cycle takes about ninety minutes. In the newborn the comparable length is only fifty minutes, and this changes little in the course of the first year. What does change radically is the proportion of REM to NREM sleep: between birth and adulthood REM sleep diminishes by about 80 per cent but NREM sleep only by 25 per cent. In the newborn the REM phase accounts for something like 60 per cent of total sleep, and there are indications that in the foetus this figure approaches 100. With increasing age, however, both the amount and ratio of REM sleep gradually diminish. The point is, though, that even in premature babies the fundamental periodicity is already clear.

Why is REM sleep so prevalent early on? What is its function? One (admittedly speculative) answer that has been given is that the considerable increase in neuronal activity and blood flow in the brain that accompanies it may be essential for normal growth of central nervous tissue. The foetus, shielded by the uterine sac, and the young baby, still relatively immobile, receive very little environmental stimulation; REM sleep may therefore serve as a built-in self-stimulating system that periodically provides the organism with activity and thus helps to prepare the central nervous system for dealing with 'real' stimulation.

Spontaneity and periodicity

However this may be, the study of sleep is important because it illustrates two essential characteristics of infant behaviour:

namely, its spontaneity and its periodicity. As far as spontaneity is concerned, the infant is by no means an inert being that is stirred into activity only through the impact of environmental stimulation. It appears rather that there are endogenous forces that regulate much of his behaviour and account for changes in his ongoing activity. It has been shown that this applies equally to his waking life: there too regular fluctuations occur in his arousal state which may in turn account for the fact that quite different responses may be produced by the same type of stimulus on different occasions. The work of Heinz Prechtl in Groningen has shown this very clearly: a paediatrician, for instance, conducting a neurological examination with a newborn will obtain confusing and misleading results if he does not note whether the infant is drowsy, alert, or in a state of high excitement. Responses cannot be explained in terms of environmental stimuli alone: the ongoing organisation will always act to mediate and modify their impact, even in the baby.

As to periodicity, it appears that the spontaneous changes that take place tend to occur in definite rhythms. The sleep-wake cycles of infants are of much shorter duration than those of adults, for the newborn wakens every three to four hours and cannot sustain wakefulness for long. But periodicity is by no means impervious to experience, and Kleitman and others have shown that very quickly within the first year of life there occurs a shift in the distribution of sleeping and waking towards the socially more acceptable diurnal pattern of the adult. It has also been shown that in brain-injured infants the cyclical nature of activity may be absent or impaired, and while this may in time rectify itself we have here a very definite indication that endogenous regulating devices exist within the central nervous system.

The same two characteristics—spontaneity and periodicity —are also evident in the infant's sucking behaviour. Sucking is far from being a simple response: it is a complex sequence of movements that shows a precise, innately organised coordination with such other responses as swallowing, breathing and the rooting reflex. It is also far from being just a reflexive reaction to certain types of stimuli. On the one hand, it regularly occurs quite spontaneously, particularly in certain kinds of arousal states; on the other hand, it may occasionally be impossible to elicit at all, even by contact with the nipple. In general sucking is often an active searching for the necessary stimulus rather than being passively elicited by action initiated by the mother.

The sucking response shows, moreover, all the characteristics of a high-frequency rhythm. It is organised on a burst-pause pattern, with the number of sucks per burst ranging from about five to twenty and the pauses between four and fifteen seconds. These patterns depend on such factors as whether sucking is spontaneous or elicited, whether it is to nutritive or non-nutritive substances, and also on a number of individual characteristics. It generally takes place, however, at a frequency of two sucks per second. There is thus a definite temporal patterning underlying the response that—as with the sleeping-waking cycle—is primarily regulated by an endogenous mechanism in the brain. Infants with congenital mouth defects show no disturbance in the cyclical organisation of sucking; in some brain-injured infants, on the other hand, the burst-pause rhythm shows marked irregularities.

The mother fits in

Individual differences in burst-pause patterns have been found which show at least some short-term consistency. They give further substance to the general point that from birth on there is already a behavioural organisation which the infant brings to any interaction situation. How the mother behaves, therefore, is every bit as much a function of the infant's characteristics as those of her own make-up. Indeed, according to Kenneth Kaye and Terry Brazelton at Harvard, it is the function of pauses between bursts of sucking to act as signals to the mother to initiate social interaction by activities such as jiggling and stroking. The timing of such stimulation is important, however, for if it comes too soon at the beginning of a

pause it is (contrary to the mother's intention) likely to retard
rather than speed up the onset of the next burst of sucks.
Sensitive mothers, it seems, do not intrude too readily in the
sequential flow of the infant's behaviour.

Infant behaviour, we can conclude, reflects the fine synchronisation endogenously determined, of different response
patterns with one another. But an infant does not exist in a
vacuum, and the integration of his responses with those of
his caretakers becomes one of the major developmental tasks
of early childhood. How is this achieved to yield the fine
temporal synchrony that characterises any smooth social interaction? Micro-analytic techniques, involving the frame-
by-frame analysis of films or video-tapes of mother-child
interaction sequences, are beginning to give us some of the
answers.

In some respects the newborn baby's behaviour is already
pre-adapted to social interaction. As the above observation by
Kaye and Brazelton shows, the periodic nature of sucking
provides the mother with an opportunity to interact with the
baby in the pauses between his responses, thereby establishing
the most basic feature of any relationship, namely an alternation in the activity of the two partners.

Alternation in vocalisation

Such alternation is indeed a widespread characteristic of mother-
infant interaction generally. In a programme of research on
the development of early interpersonal synchronicity which
my colleagues and I are pursuing, we have, for instance, been
repeatedly struck by the turn-taking nature of mother's and
baby's vocalisations. Mother and baby rarely vocalise at the
same time, and the alternation so produced is thus somewhat
like a conversation among adults. Some people suggest that
this is a built-in phenomenon reflecting a limit on information
processing, in that one cannot easily speak and listen at the
same time, and that infants are thus from the beginning
equipped to 'give the other person a turn'. However, another
(and to me much more likely) explanation is that the turn-
taking is entirely due to the mother's initiative. The baby, in

other words, emits bursts of vocalisations, and it is left to the mother to fill in the pauses. What one then observes is a synchronisation of the two sets of responses which in fact does not yet reflect a true social reciprocity but is entirely due to the mother letting herself be paced by the infant's periodic behaviour.

Visual synchrony

This conclusion is also suggested by another of our studies (undertaken by Glyn Collis and myself) in which we examined the synchrony to be found between the mother's and the baby's visual responses. That mutual gazing or 'eye contact' plays an important part in social interaction is widely accepted, and much has been written about the way in which looking may function as a signal and about its integration with other responses such as vocalising and bodily movement. But however important face-to-face interaction may be, one must also bear in mind that interaction is frequently of an indirect nature: it takes place via features of the environment such as toys, utensils, or more distant surroundings, and that this may apply particularly to infants as yet incapable of verbal interchange.

With this in mind, we have been observing the visual behaviour of mothers and their babies in a strange environment (an observation room in our laboratory) where the baby sits on the mother's knee and we video-tape from behind a one-way window. The room is bare except for a number of large, brightly coloured and prominently placed toys. When we then analyse the video-taped records (and to do so it is necessary to use one-tenth of a second time units) we can establish two facts. In the first place, the visual responses of the participants are by no means independent of one another: rather, there is a highly significant tendency for the two to be looking at the same object at the same time. And in the second place, when we then analyse the temporal course of their visual behaviour we find that it is almost invariably the baby who leads and the mother who follows. The baby, that is, looks at the various toys in turn and the mother closely and often most sensitively follows him visually. She thus regards the baby's looking behaviour as a signal and allows her own looking behaviour to be determined by it.

Synchrony in other channels

We have here an illustration of the way in which mother and baby can share by visual means an interest in some feature of their surroundings—an interest instigated by the baby but made mutual thanks to the mother's willingness to be paced by the infant's activity. An extensive interaction sequence may then be set in train, for often the mother not only follows the baby's gaze visually but may also point to the object, name it, and talk about it. By thus linking particular verbal descriptions to the infant's visual input, a context is provided in which semantic learning can take place. The visual-visual synchrony established between mother and infant may therefore lead to further synchronisation of behaviour via other channels of communication.

The phenomenon which I have just described is of interest because it suggests a picture of early social interaction that is rather different from the traditional conception of the socialisation process. This sees the infant as passive and entirely under the direction of the mother's influence. Analogous to the imprinting process in precocial birds as described by Konrad Lorenz and other ethologists, it is the mother who is said to lead and the infant who follows. In the situation observed by us it is, on the contrary, the infant who, by visual means, leads the mother. Right up to the end of the first year infants were rarely found to follow the mother's looking behaviour. The baby's visual responses, in other words, have signal value to the mother, but for his part the infant (in this situation at least) remains a largely egocentric creature. The couple's synchrony does not yet reflect true reciprocity.

Intentional signalling

There are a number of indications in our ongoing work that such reciprocity appears only at the very end of the first year of life. Only then will the infant become capable of a number of cognitive achievements that participation in a reciprocal relationship requires: an understanding of the difference between self-produced and other-produced behaviour; an awareness of the feedback contingencies of self-produced behaviour; the capacity to modify, inhibit, and otherwise regulate responses in the light of such feedback; and the ability to anticipate the likely outcome of one's behaviour on the basis of previous experience. Up to this point, synchrony was achieved because the mother was able to endow the infant's behaviour with meaning: his cry, for instance, was a signal which mobilised her into action. From now on the infant can use signals intentionally: he no longer merely cries because he has a pain but cries in order to summon mother to his side. Once this has been accomplished social interaction may not become any more synchronised than it already is but it does become vastly more complex.

Are mothers stimulating?
ANTHONY COSTELLO

It is easy to forget that the concern with infancy that characterises contemporary western society is a relatively recent phenomenon. Until the present century a high infant mortality rate
coupled with high fertility may well have devalued the importance of a baby in the family until he had reached an age when
his security of tenure could be seen as established. Certainly,
Freud's emphasis on the significance of infantile behaviour
and mother-infant relationships preceded any direct interest
in infancy and this attitude of indifference persisted for a surprisingly long time.

As late as 1938 Wayne and Marsena Dennis of the University
of Virginia were able to publish an account of their fostering of
a pair of fraternal twins. Believing that development was the
result of maturation and unrelated to the child's activities, they
set out to test their theory by rearing these children from the
first to the fourteenth month of life in one room, neither
speaking to nor playing with the children until they were seven
months old. Their movements were restricted and they were
separated by a screen and unable to see anything except the
minimum of furnishings the room contained, and the sky
through the window. The only toys they were given in the
whole of the experiment were rattles, introduced on the 341st
day. Such an experiment is unthinkable today, and indeed a
more recent attempt to rear a child in a similarly restricted
environment for experimental reasons caused a professional
uproar.

Psychologists and parents now more or less take for granted
the concept that maternal stimulation of babies is desirable.
The syllogisms responsible run something like this: (1) babies
are adversely affected by separation from their mothers;
(2) mothers play with their babies; (3) babies are therefore
adversely affected by lack of play. Or, alternatively: (1) middle-

class parents have clever children; (2) middle-class parents stimulate their babies; (3) stimulating babies therefore makes them into clever children. No doubt there are others.

The evidence that maternal behaviour in infancy promotes 'intelligent' behaviour is surprisingly scanty. Any discussion of this topic must start with the reminder that the difficult concept of intelligence is a non-starter in infancy. In older children (and in adults) the concept of intelligence, as a quality associated with achievements in intellectual activities, has some meaning and an attempt can be made to validate intelligence scales in the way Alfred Binet began, by relating them to school performance.

In infancy, and indeed until the age of six or seven, there are no established concurrent criteria to validate any scale that can be constructed. There are, of course, a number of graded scales which can be used to describe an individual infant's behaviour in relation to a reference (standardisation) population, but psychologists are generally too cautious now to grace these with any more grandiose name than 'developmental tests'. As with intelligence tests, raw scores on these scales correlate very highly with age, though to assign a 'mental age' does not do justice to the way in which the scales are constructed. Though the scales differ in many details, nearly all rest heavily on Arnold Gesell's observations and material which date from the mid 1920s.

These similarities may account for the almost uniform finding of many studies that performance on developmental tests in the first three years of life bears little or no relationship to subsequent IQ scores in later childhood. The only caveat to be made is that many of the children with very low scores are in the lowest IQ ranges later on, and that amongst those with slightly higher scores an experienced clinician may be able to identify on medical criteria a further group who later prove to be well below average in IQ.

It seems a paradox that marked differences in the sorts of behaviour in infancy which look intelligent, in the sense that a proud parent might say 'There's a clever boy' if the child achieved the task, are not related to differences in tasks with similar face validity in later life. If we conceive of growth as a sequence in which mastery of one step prepares the foundation for the next (a convenient oversimplification of Piaget's theories of cognitive development) there is no logical reason to suppose that a snapshot impression of the current preoccupations of the child must tell us something about the rate at which he will progress to a later stage in the sequence, when he is concerned with mental operations of a very different type.

There is some support for this view from a re-analysis of one of the early longitudinal studies. James Cameron and Norman Livson of the University of California, looking at Nancy Bayley's data on 74 children whom she followed for a period of 25 years, were able to show that the ratings of vocal behaviour of the children, observed in a test situation in infancy, were the only items in the test which correlated with later IQ. The significance of this finding is that infant vocalisation can readily be increased by experimental reinforcement schedules— in other words, a characteristic which predicts later attainment is known to be subject to early environmental influences.

Need for favourable environment

Bayley also made detailed ratings of maternal behaviour in infancy, but the relationship between these measures and test scores, both in infancy and later childhood, is not clear cut; there are inconsistencies and puzzling sex differences and the relationships are so small that they only hover on the borderline of what might be expected to be found by chance alone. Other authors report similar findings and although it is possible to conclude that responsive, warm and stimulating mothers do not damage a child's intellectual development, such a conclusion is neither interesting nor helpful.

Longitudinal studies are further limited by the logical difficulty that the same parents generally rear the children throughout childhood, so that ratings of mothers in infancy may be measuring characteristics which are most important in nurturing intellectual development at a later stage. The tendency to overlook this possibility has been fostered by the misconceived but widely held notion that fifty per cent of a child's mental growth is achieved by the age of five; this figure is derived from an analysis of correlations between IQ measured at different ages, and the finding is that at most fifty per cent of the later variance in IQ scores can be accounted for by test results at five, which is a rather different statement. As Professor A. D. B. Clarke of Hull University has cogently argued, there is no real reason to suppose that environmental influences on development are most important in early childhood. The disappointing lack of long-term effects from various 'enrichment programmes' for deprived children is as well explained by an ongoing need for a favourable environment as by Jensen's argument that the poor achievement of deprived children is genetically determined. The neatest experimental solutions to these difficulties would involve morally unacceptable manipulations of children's lives.

The psychologist who is interested in individual differences thus seems to be driven into a corner with no strategy to help him escape. I believe there are escape routes, though the paths are tortuous. One is to concentrate on a more refined and careful analysis of the abilities of young children, in the way Tom Bower and Genevieve Carpenter describe (see Chapters 11 and 12). Another is to start from the proposition that existing infant tests do record a wide range of behaviours in which there is great variation from one individual to another and to explore the reasons for this variation. Some part of it is undoubtedly genetically determined.

Dan Freedman, of Chicago, studied the social responses of an infant to an adult, using a group of twins seen at frequent intervals in the first year of life. He filmed each twin's behaviour separately and then had each record scored by separate groups of judges using Bayley's infant behaviour profile. These independent records showed that identical twins were substantially more alike than fraternals both in the quality and in the quantity of such behaviours as smiling, vocalising, and attending to mother and experimenter, and in the time at which changes in these behaviours emerged.

R. S. Wilson has reported similar results using the motor

and mental scales of the Bayley test on a large group of twins from the Louisville twin study who are being followed longitudinally. Identical twins show fewer within-pair differences in developmental status than fraternal twins. Moreover, the fluctuations in relative status from one occasion to the next also seem to have a large genetic element. If one member of a twin pair scores lower on one occasion than he did three months before, his twin is more likely to show a similarly lowered score if the pair are identical than if they are fraternal. Although estimates of heritability have to be hedged round with qualifications it seems likely that at least half, and possibly a little more, of the variation in infant test scores is genetically determined, assuming that the range of environmental conditions is restricted to that which existed in the populations that have been studied.

Observing interactions

My own approach to the environmental variables in this equation has been to avoid, as far as possible, the subjective rating of parental behaviour. Although it is possible to show that judges can be trained so that they can rate independently but agree closely on such qualities as maternal warmth or responsiveness, this demonstration shows only that two people can be trained to use the same but possibly biassed rules, and says nothing about the validity of the rating. Direct observation of mother-child interaction is possibly less open to bias, but the limitations of the human observer restrict the number of behaviours that can be observed.

The more miniscule the behaviour is, the easier it is to define it in operational terms, but the most ambitious exponents of direct observation have rarely used more than some eighty categories of behaviour, and most have used far fewer. Inevitably there is selection for what is conceived as worthwhile observing, and it is a nice point to decide if the weaknesses of global ratings are greater than the difficulties of making an appropriate selection of small behaviour items and drawing together the data obtained into a meaningful pattern. My colleagues and I have attempted a short cut by arguing that if maternal behaviour is to have an effect, the amount of it is as important as the quality, and that it is more likely that mothers whose behaviour fosters desired behaviour in the infant will spend more time with their babies than that 'bad' or unsuccessful mothers will spend just as much time doing the 'wrong' things. This makes sense both from the clinical viewpoint and from an alternative behaviourist analysis of the pay-off involved for mothers, and is only likely to fall down if we have very different interpretations of the aims of child rearing from our subjects.

Our aim therefore has been to obtain quantitative estimates of the distribution of a mother's time between her children and other activities, and estimates of the amount of time a child spends in a fairly simply defined range of categories of behaviour. The basic tool for this was developed in this unit by James Douglas, Annette Lawson, John Cooper and Elizabeth Cooper. The technique used is to interview a mother about the detailed events of the preceding twenty-four hours, using a flexible open-ended interviewing technique designed to elicit as much detail as is necessary to determine the where-abouts of each individual in the household and his or her activities at that time, breaking the day down into intervals rounded to the nearest five minutes. The interview is tape recorded, transcribed and coded from the transcript. From the coded data it is an easy step to produce computer-generated summaries of the amount of time spent by each individual in certain broad categories. In this way we can determine, for example, the amount of time each child was playing, sleeping, crying or eating, or held by his mother or father, or in the same room as an adult. It is possible to validate these measures by direct observation, and by other techniques.

My colleague Norman Hoare has developed electronic devices to monitor some aspects of mother/child behaviour, using such behavioural variables as the physical activity of the baby, the nature of sounds in his vicinity, and the proximity of the mother to the baby. Although these devices are as yet restricted to babies in the cot—and their development is incomplete—we have corroborative evidence from records of the child's activity in the cot that the mother's account of when the child was placed in the cot or removed, and when he went to sleep or woke up, is substantially correct, and that though she may make errors in estimation of the exact time, her estimates of duration when summed over twenty-four hours are remarkably accurate.

Hazards at birth

We have used these measures to study various aspects of infancy. Preliminary results on a small random sample of 60 six-month-old first-born children suggests that by combining these with relatively crude scales of the hazards of delivery and the neonatal period, we can account for a reasonable proportion of the variation in developmental status in six months. Juggling with a number of variables in this way is notoriously tricky. We have to follow up the subsequent development of these children, and replicate the original study, before we can be sure that this is not just a chance relationship, plausible though the findings appear.

The same technique can be used to study situations which are known to be associated with statistically abnormal but not necessarily handicapping outcomes. Twins have commonly been studied in the way I outlined earlier to elucidate problems of inheritance. Although it has long been known that the development of twins in some respects follows a different pattern from the development of singleton children, this aspect of twinning has been relatively neglected. As long ago as 1932 Ella Day reported from the Institute of Child Welfare at Minnesota, where so much of the early work on child development began, that twins were slightly behind singletons in intelligence at the age of five, and showed a much more striking delay in language development, a delay which appeared to increase from the second to the fifth year.

Later studies confirmed the language discrepancy, though more recent work, such as that of Peter Mittler, who surveyed

200 four-year-old twins in Buckinghamshire, has not shown such marked delays and there is evidence that twins catch up in language ability during the school years. The effect is still detectable on the verbal scales of the now largely discarded eleven-plus tests, and R. G. Record and Thomas McKeown at Birmingham used the eleven-plus results of 50,000 children for whom they also had obstetric records to show that the survivors in twinships, when one twin had died at or soon after birth, had verbal scores approaching those of single-born children. This suggests that the physical hazards of twin pregnancies and deliveries are not responsible for the language delays of twins.

Penelope Leach and I began a longitudinal study of twins to explore the differences in the mother's behaviour, and to look at the differences in the environment between twins and single-born children. It is a hazard of twin studies that the relative rarity of twins means either that the sample is scattered over a large area, or that it takes a long time to collect, and although this work began some years ago it will not be until the end of this year that we can start to analyse findings on the whole of the sample. It is, however, already possible to examine differences between the care of first-born twins and first-born singletons when they are six months old. Despite the burden of mothering twins, mothers of twins spend overall little more time on activities directly concerned with the babies. The inevitable result is that much more of a mother's time with a twin is spent on the basic essentials of feeding, changing and bathing, and much less in play. Although fathers of twins do contribute more time to the care of twins, the overall contribution is very small compared with the mother's time. The amount of time each twin is held is little more than half the time that a singleton is held, and other measures of individual maternal attention are correspondingly reduced.

The interpretation of this finding will depend on relating it to differences in development within and between pairs. But already it is tempting to suppose that this dilution of maternal attention may be responsible for the delays in a twin's

growth of language, rather than the influence of one twin on
the other and the development of private language which has
been adduced as a reason by many workers in this field. Indeed,
our own data from a survey of twins and singletons near their
third birthday suggests that true private language is relatively
uncommon, though twins tend to spend a little longer in the
phase of neologisms and 'baby language' than single-born
children. There may of course be compensating subtleties of
nonverbal communication, though there is little work on the
relationship of individual differences in the two modes of
communicating. It seems quite likely that good verbal communicators may also be good nonverbal communicators.
Certainly it is difficult to find concrete evidence that twins
communicate more efficiently, rather than more readily, with
each other than with adults or other children.

I have unashamedly concentrated on individual differences
in cognitive development. Some psychologists have argued
that the whole notion of IQ is socially divisive and should be
abandoned. To my mind this is not only a Luddite aim which,
if realised, would leave unsatisfied an appetite for information
whetted by the incomplete findings psychologists have so far
been able to produce, but one which ignores the immense
value our society places on intelligent behaviour and the practical implications which follow. If we were to reject intelligence as a key characteristic in the social structure it seems
only too likely that we would fall back to a more oppressive
society. Intelligence is a concept which has been used too
narrowly and over-emphasised to the point where other valuable personal qualities have been overlooked. Nevertheless,
unless we can achieve such a revolution that no differentiation of responsibility is needed in our society (an unlikely
Utopia) ability to reason and understand seems a better
criterion for selecting leaders than most of the others that
human societies have used.

CHILDREN AT PLAY

Until ethologists discovered the importance of play in the maturation of the higher primates, the topic remained largely neglected by psychologists interested in human development.

It is through play that children learn about their environment. Play is important in the acquisition of certain basic skills; it is instrumental in early language acquisition; and it conveys certain cultural attributes to the child. The degree of imagination in self-directed play in young children is an index to (and an influence on?) imagination and creativity in childhood.

The importance of play
JEROME BRUNER

Experimental psychology tends to be rather a sober discipline, tough-minded not only in its procedures, but in its choice of topics as well. They must be scientifically manageable. No surprise, then, that when it began extending its investigations into the realm of early human development it steered clear of so antic a phenomenon as play. For even as recently as a few decades ago, Harold Schlosberg of Brown University, a highly respected critic, published a carefully reasoned paper concluding sternly that, since play could not even be properly defined, it could scarcely be a manageable topic for experimental research. His paper was not without merit, for the phenomena of play cannot be impeccably framed into a single operational definition. How indeed can one encompass so motley a set of entries as childish punning, cowboys-and-indians, and the construction of a tower of bricks, into a single or even a sober dictionary entry?

Play harnessed
Fortunately, the progress of research is subject to accidents of opportunity. Once data begin seriously to undermine presuppositions, the course can change very quickly. A decade ago, while Schlosberg's words still reverberated, work on primate ethology began to force a change in direction, raising new and basic questions about the nature and role of play in the evolution of the primate series. On closer inspection, play is not as diverse a phenomenon as had been thought, particularly when looked at in its natural setting. Nor is it that all antic in its structure, if analysed properly. But perhaps most important, its role during immaturity appears to be more and more central as one moves up the living primate series from Old World monkeys through Great Apes, to Man—suggesting that in the evolution of primates, marked by an increase in the number

of years of immaturity, the selection of a capacity for play during those years may have been crucial. So if play seemed to the methodologically vexed to be an unmanageable laboratory topic, primatologists were pondering its possible centrality in evolution!

A first field finding served to reduce the apparently dizzying variety of forms that play could take. On closer inspection, it turns out that play is universally accompanied in subhuman primates by a recognisable form of metasignalling, a 'play face', first carefully studied by the Dutch primatologist J.A.R.A.M. van Hooff. It signifies within the species the message, to use Gregory Bateson's phrase, 'this is play'. It is a powerful signal — redundant in its features, which include a particular kind of open-mouthed gesture, a slack but exaggerated gait, and a marked 'galumphing' in movement — and its function is plainly not to be understood simply as 'practice of instinctive activities crucial for survival'. When, for example, Stephen Miller and I set about analysing filmed field records of juvenile play behaviour made by Irven DeVore while studying Savanna baboons in the Amboseli Game Reserve in East Africa, we very quickly discovered that if one young animal did not see the 'metasignal' of another who was seeking to play-fight with him, a real fight broke out with no lack of skill. But once the signal was perceived by both parties the fight was transformed into the universally recognisable clownish ballet of monkeys feigning a fight. They obviously knew how to do it both ways. What was it for, then, play fighting? And why should the accompanying form of metasignalling have been selected in evolution?

We begin to get a hint of the functional significance of play in higher primates from the pioneering observations of the group led by Jane vanLawick-Goodall studying free-ranging chimpanzees at the Gombe Stream Reserve in Tanzania. Recall first the considerably longer childhood in chimpanzees than in Old World monkeys — the young chimp in close contact with the mother for four or five years during which the mother has no other offspring, whilst in monkeys, the oestrus cycle assures that within a year new young are born, with the rapidly maturing animals of last year's crop relegated to a peer group of juveniles in which play declines rapidly.

Observation and play

David Hamburg of Stanford, a psychiatrist-primatologist working at Gombe Stream, has noted the extent to which young chimpanzees in the first five years spend time observing adult behaviour, incorporating observed patterns of adult behaviour into their play. Janevan Lawick-Goodall has a telling observation to report that relates this early observation-cum-play to adult skilled behaviour—an observation that deepens our understanding of the function of early play. Adult chimps develop (when the ecology permits) a very skilled technique of termiting, in which they put mouth-wetted, stripped sticks into the opening of a termite hill, wait a bit for the termites to adhere to the stick, then carefully remove their fishing 'instrument' with termites adhering to it which they then eat with relish. One of the young animals, Merlin, lost his mother in his third year. He had not learned to termite by four-and-a-half nearly as well as the others, though raised by older siblings. For the young animals appear to learn the 'art of termiting' by sitting by the mother, buffered from pressures, trying out in play and learning the individual constituent acts that make up termiting, and without the usual reinforcement of food from catching: learning to play with sticks, to strip leaves from twigs, and to pick the right length of twig for getting into different holes. These are the constituents that must be combined in the final act, and they are tried out in all manner of antic episodes.

Merlin, compared to his age mates, was inept and unequipped. He had not had the opportunity for such observation and play nor, probably, did he get the buffering from distraction and pressure normally provided by the presence of a mother. This would suggest, then, that play has the effect not so much of providing practice of survival-relevant instinctive behaviour, but rather of making possible the playful practice of subroutines of behaviour later to be combined in more useful problem solving. What appears to be at stake in play is the opportunity for assembling and reassembling behaviour sequences for skilled action. That, at least, is one function of play.

Moratorium on frustration

It suggests a more general feature of play. It is able to reduce or neutralise the pressure of goal-directed action, the 'push' to successful completion of an act. There is a well known rule in the psychology of learning, the Yerkes-Dodson law, that states that the more complex a skill to be learned, the lower the *optimum* motivational level required for fastest learning. Play, then, may provide the means for reducing excessive drive. The distinguished Russian investigator Lev Vygotsky in a long-lost manuscript published a few years ago reports an investigation in which young children could easily be induced not to eat their favourite candy when laid before them when the candy was made part of a game of 'Poison'. And years before (in 1925) Wolfgang Köhler reported that when his chimps were learning to stack boxes to reach fruit suspended from the high tops of their cages, they often lost interest in eating the fruit when they were closing in on the solution. Indeed Peter Reynolds, in a widely acclaimed paper on play in primates given to the American Association for the Advancement of Science in Washington, DC, in 1972, remarks that the essence of play is to dissociate goal-directed behaviour from its principal drive system and customary reinforcements. It is no surprise, then, to find results indicating that prior play with materials improves children's problem solving with those materials later.

Kathy Sylva and Paul Genova of Harvard and I worked with children aged three to five who had the task of fishing a prize from a latched box out of reach. To do so, they had to extend two sticks by clamping them together. The children were given various 'training' procedures beforehand, including demonstration of the principle of clamping two sticks together, or practice in fastening clamps on single sticks, or an opportu-

nity to watch the experimenter carry out the task. One group
was simply allowed to play with the materials. They did as
well in solving the problem as the ones who had been given
a demonstration of the principle of clamping sticks together
and better than any of the other groups. The table summarises
the differences between the groups (each 36 in number, equally
divided between three-, four-, and five-year-olds) in terms of
number of spontaneous solutions with no aid from the
experimenter.

Prior Training	*Percent Spontaneous Solution*
Play with materials	40
Observation of complete solution	41
Observation of components of solution	18
Instructed manipulation of materials	20
No training	8

The difference between the 'play' group and the 'complete
solution' group is insignificant, and both are reliably better
than all the other groups. In fact, what was striking about the
play group was their tenacity in sticking with the task so that
even when they were poor in their initial approach, they ended
by solving the problem. What was particularly striking was
their capacity to resist frustration and 'giving up'. They were
playing.

Youth is more inventive
There are comparable results on primates below man where
the pressure is taken off animals by other means—as by semi-
domestication achieved by putting out food in a natural habitat,
a technique pioneered by Japanese primatologists. It appears
to have the effect of increasing innovation in the animals
studied. Japanese macaques at Takasakiyama have taken to
washing yams, to separating maize from the sand on which it
is spread by dropping a handful of the mix into seawater and
letting the sand sink. And once in the water, playing in this
new medium to the edge of which they have been transplanted,

the young learn to swim, first in play, and then beginning to swim off, migrating to near islands. In all of these activities, it is the playful young who are centrally involved in the new enterprises, even if they may not always be the innovators of the new 'technologies'. But it is the young who are game for a change, and it is this gameness that predisposes the troop to change in ways—with the fully adult males often the most resistant, or at least the most out of touch, for the novelties are being tried out in the groups playing around the mother from which the big males are absent. Jean Claude Fady, the French primatologist, has shown that even ordinarily combative adult males will cooperate with each other in moving heavy rocks under which food is hidden—if the pressure is taken off by the technique of semi-domestication.

Ample early opportunity for play may have a more lasting effect still, as Corinne Hutt has shown. She designed a super-toy for children of three to five years old, consisting of a table with a lever, buzzer, bells and counters, different movements of the lever systematically sounding buzzers, and turning counters, etcetera. Children first explore its possibilities, then having contented themselves, often proceed to play. She was able to rate how inventive the children were in their play, dividing them into non-explorers, explorers, and inventive explorers, the last group carrying on all the way from initial exploration to full-blown play. Four years later, when the children were aged seven to ten, she tested them again on a creativity test designed by Mike Wallach and Nathan Kogan in the United States, as well as on some personality tests.

The more inventive and exploratory the children had been initially in playing with the super-toy, the higher their originality scores were four years later. The non-exploring boys in general had come to view themselves as unadventurous and inactive and their parents and teachers considered them as lacking curiosity. The non-exploratory and unplayful girls were later rather unforthcoming in social interaction as well and more tense than their originally more playful mates. Early unplayfulness may go with a lack of later originality.

Obviously, more studies of this kind are needed (and are in

progress). But the psychiatrist Erik Erikson, reporting in his Goldkin Lectures at Harvard in 1973 on a thirty-year follow-up of children earlier studied, has commented that the ones with the most interesting and fulfilling lives were the ones who had managed to keep a sense of playfulness at the centre of things.

Play has rules

Consider play now from a structural point of view as a form of activity. Rather than being 'random' it is usually found to be characterised by a recognisable rule structure.

New studies by the young American psycholinguist Catherine Garvey show how three- to five-year-old children, playing in pairs, manage implicitly even in their simplest games to create and recognise rules and expectancies, managing the while to distinguish sharply between the structure of make-believe or possibility and the real thing.

Here is one example, one in which the rule is to respond identically:

First Child	*Second Child*
Bye Mummy	
	Bye Mummy
Bye Mummy	
	Bye Daddy
You're a nut	
	No I'm not

In other rounds, a complement rule prevails, and the expected response is indeed 'Bye Daddy' in reaction to the first child's 'Bye Mummy'. The rules also specify recognition of the situation in which the play is set, as in the example:

I have to go to work	
	You're already at work
No I'm not	

But withal, children at this age are quite aware of the line between fantasy and reality, as in the following example when one child sits down on a three-legged stool with a magnifying glass at its centre:

I've got to go to the potty

                        (Turns to him) Really?

(Grins) No, pretend

Amusing though these protocols may be, they reveal a concise, almost grammatical quality in the interchanges and an extraordinary sensitivity on the part of the children to violations of implicit expectancies and codes.

It is hardly surprising then that different cultures encourage different forms of play as 'fitting'. Ours tend, in the main, to admire play and games of 'zero sum', one wins what the other loses. The anthropologist Kenelm Burridge contrasts our favourite form with a typical ritual food-exchange game of 'taketak' among the Tangu in New Guinea, a tribe that practises strict and equal sharing. The object of their game is to achieve equal shares among the players—not to win, not to lose, but to tie. It is reminiscent of a game reported years ago by James Sully. He tells of two sisters, five and seven, who played a game they called 'Sisters', a game with one rule: equal shares for each player, no matter what, in their case quite unlike life! Or, in Garvey's protocols.

First Child	*Second Child*
Coffee too?	
	No, I'm a little boy
	I'll have some milk
OK You can eat now	
	(Moves closer to stove)
Kid, we're going to get some milk from the store	

We are only at the beginning of studying the functions of play in fitting children to their culture, but there are some classic studies.

Play and language development

If the rule structure of human play and games sensitises
the child to the rules of culture, both generally and in preparation for a particular way of life, then surely play must have some
special role in nurturing symbolic activity generally. For culture
is symbolism in action. Does play then have some deep connection with the origins of language? One can never know.
Yet, we have already noted the extraordinary combinatorial
push behind play, its working out of variations. Play is certainly
implicated in early language acquisition. Its structured interactions and 'rules' precede and are a part of the child's first
mastery of language. Our own studies at Oxford on language
acquisition suggest that in exchange games, in 'peep-bo', and
in other structured interactions, young children learn to signal
and to recognise signals and expectancies. They delight in
primitive rule structures that come to govern their encounters.
In these encounters, they master the idea of 'privileges of
occurrence' so central to grammar, as well as other constituents
of language that must later be put together.

One set of episodes from our studies illustrates how play
serves as a vehicle for language acquisition. Nan at nine
months has begun to signal in an exchange game when she
gives an object to her mother, using *Kew* (a version of 'Thank
you'). She has not yet learned the language code for giving and
receiving, although she has learned the rules for the game.
In three months, the demonstrative *Look* has replaced *Kew* in
the giving phase, and *Kew* has moved into its correct receiving
position in the sequence. Nan has used the correct serial order
in the play to sort out the correct order in the language that
accompanies the play.

> (Nine months, two weeks) Give-and-take game. Child offers
> book to Mother and then withdraws it when Mother reaches
> for it, with the Child showing great excitement. Hands book
> to Mother, saying *Kew* when Mother takes it.

> (Ten months, two weeks) Child plays with blocks. Says
> *Kew* when offering block to camera operators. Not observed

ever to say *Kew* when receiving block or any object. Give-and-take game always involves Nan saying *Kew* when handing block to Mother.

(Twelve months, two weeks) Mother hands Child ring. Now Child says *Kew* when receiving. Three minutes later Child hands Mother a toy postbox, a favourite. Child says *Look* when handing.

Indeed, there is a celebrated and highly technical volume by Ruth Weir on language play in a two-and-one-half-year-old child, *Language in the Crib,* in which she reports on the language of her son Anthony after he had been put to bed with lights out. He pushes combinatorial activity to the limit, phonologically, syntactically, and semantically, often to the point at which he remonstrates himself with an adult 'Oh no, no'.

Much more is being learned about play than we would have expected a decade ago. We have come a long way since Piaget's brilliant observations in the mid 1940s on the role of play in assimilating the child's experience to his personal schema of the world, as preparation for later accommodation to it. A new period of research on play is underway. Nick Blurton-Jones has shown that Niko Tinbergen's ethological methods can be applied to children at play as readily as to chimps in the forest. The new work begins to suggest why play is the principal business of childhood, the vehicle of improvisation and combination, the first carrier of rule systems through which a world of cultural restraint is substituted for the operation of impulse.

That such research as that reported raises deep questions about the role of play in our own society is, of course, self-evident. Although we do not yet know how important play is for growing up, we do know that it is serious business. How serious it is can perhaps be condensed by citing the conclusion of a study reported in 1972 on children's laughter by Alan Sroufe and his colleagues at Minnesota. They find that those things most likely to make a child laugh when done by his mother at a year are most likely to make him cry when done by a stranger.

LANGUAGE

Of all the basic skills possessed by humans, the one that most separates him from the rest of the animal kingdom is language.

Psychologists are interested in how young infants manage the remarkable feat of acquiring what is an amazingly complex mental activity: how much of language is taught and how much is innate—this question is at the heart of research on language. There are signs that infants just a few months old make positive attempts to speak, an activity that has been called pre-speech. And it seems that newborn babies respond specifically to the sound of a human voice.

Early attempts at speech

COLWYN TREVARTHEN

Some years ago I began to study infants with the intention of looking for signs of what innate structure of intelligence lay dormant or weakly expressed in them—a biological gift to the beginning human being. I knew that human newborns possess huge, elaborate brains, but they were credited with doing very little; this puzzled me. With the aid of modern recording techniques, but especially television and film, I soon obtained data that made me suspect that much of the innate pattern of human intention and a predisposition to perceive and use the world, including people, had been glossed over in scientific studies of infants. Most remarkable were indications that infants of a few weeks of age were showing signs of intentions to *speak* and that soon after this they were entering into well-organised, sometimes even witty or humorous, conversation-like exchanges with adults.

The film project

In a preliminary film study Martin Richards and I, working with Jerome Bruner at Harvard, sought to determine if and when infants developed behaviours indicating that they perceived things and people differently. We filmed five babies once a week from birth until they were six months old, either with a small toy suspended nearly in front of them, or with their mother.

This method of contrasting observations did indeed bring to light strong differences in the innate behaviour of infants. We saw highly elaborate activity that was specific to communicating with persons in all subjects while they were with their mothers. The mother was simply asked to 'chat with her baby', and no mother thought this an odd request. Her presence, what she looked like, the way she moved, the sounds she made, evoked in babies, even those a few weeks old, behaviours that were different from those they made a moment later to the suspended object. The infant showed two different kinds of interest, two ways of spontaneously responding; one for the object, and one for the mother. Most different were the expressions of face, voice and hands.

We hypothesised two modes of psychological action: communication with persons; and 'doing' with objects. The latter included visually exploring and tracking, trying to grasp, trying to kick or step on, or trying to seize in the mouth (Figure 1).

Figure 1   Arm and hand movements of innate "prereaching" in a three-week-old baby; he follows the moving object with eye and head. The rudimentary reaching movements occur at a rate close to that of the unconsciously regulated adult reach-and-grasp. Eyes-head-arms-hands and legs and feet are linked in a single system that can be aimed to places in nearby spaces round the baby's body. The distance of the object is critical, even though the reach is too short and fails to touch the object.

The pattern of movement shown in this picture is representa-
tive of 'intending' which other persons may 'understand'. I
believe it is essential to analyse the form and cadence of spontaneous acts like this, and especially their selective orientation
to events in the field, if we are to comprehend how infants
identify persons and communicate with them. The perceptual
capacities of young infants brought to light by Tom Bower's
work (see Chapter 11) and particularly the evidence for a
special perception of the human face reviewed by Genevieve
Carpenter (see Chapter 12) must be involved in the behaviours
we observe, but I think the detection of animate movement
and its direction is primary for establishment of interpersonal
communication.

Unchanging pacemakers

In one of our present research projects we have been examining
the directedness of various parts of the infant's body within a
coherent space frame—orientation of eyes, ears, hands and feet
to events near the baby—and we have also been measuring
innate rhythms manifest in this orienting. A discovery of
major importance is that the basic pacemakers of attending
and intending movements in infants operate at frequencies in
time that are the same as those of adults (Figure 2). This means
that when a newborn is alert and coordinated, its still very
rudimentary movements have, nevertheless, the pace as well
as the form of activities such as looking, listening, and reaching
to touch, from the start. This can be perceived and reacted to
unconsciously by an older person. As the person approaches
the infant, acting gently and carefully as people tend to do
instinctively to a baby, then all the emanations from this
approach have rhythmical properties that are comparable with
those inside the movement-generating mechanisms of the
infant's brain. From this correspondence I believe the infant
builds a bridge to persons. Here we touch on the same topic
as that raised by the remarkable observations of rhythmic
coordination which William Condon reports (see Chapter 8).
The data of Martin Richards and Judy Bernal show that reci-

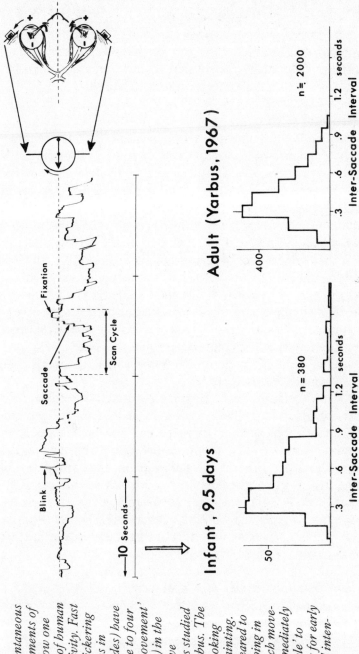

Figure 2 Spontaneous looking movements of a newborn show one basic rhythm of human voluntary activity. Fast side-to-side flickering of the two eyes in unison (saccades) have the same three to four per second 'movement' (as in a watch) in the baby and in five Russian adults studied by Alfred Yarbus. The adults were looking over a large painting. The baby appeared to be seeing nothing in particular. Such movements are immediately 'understandable' to adults looking for early signs of visual intention in babies.

Blink

Saccade

Fixation

Scan Cycle

10 Seconds

Infant, 9.5 days

n = 380

Inter-Saccade Interval

.3   .6   .9   1.2   seconds

50

Adult (Yarbus, 1967)

n ≐ 2000

Inter-Saccade Interval

.3   .6   .9   1.2   seconds

400

procal communication between a newborn and the mother is instrumental in establishing an effective relationship of care, and that deficiencies of responsiveness or expression on either part may have lasting effects on their relationship.

Prespeech

Since coming to Edinburgh I have begun a detailed examination of infant communication with persons in a project supported by the Social Science Research Council. With Penelope Hubley and Lynne Murray, I have made films, analysis of which reveals that the acts of two-month-olds responding to attentions of other persons outline many psychological processes of talking between adults. We have found activity which is best called 'prespeech' because both the context in which it occurs and its form indicate that it is a rudimentary form of speaking by movements of lips and tongue (Figures 3 and 4). These distinctive movements are often made by young infants soundlessly. At other times young babies are very vocal, making a variety of cooing sounds as they move mouth and tongue. We note a specific pattern of breathing with prespeech even when sounds are not made.

Also associated with prespeech are distinctive 'hand-waving' movements that are developmentally related to the gestures or gesticulations of adults in 'eager' and 'graphic' conversation (Figures 3 and 4). We are now sure that, notwithstanding the importance of cultural development in the formation of language, both of speech and of gestures, the foundation for interpersonal communication between humans is 'there' at birth, and is remarkably useful by eight weeks when cognitive and memory processes are just starting on the path to mastery of the world of physical events.

Communication is the essence

We can now confidently say that communication activity is much more complex than any other form of activity of infants at this age. We conclude that human intelligence develops from the start as an interpersonal process and that the maturation of consciousness and the ability to act with voluntary control in the physical world is a product rather than an ingredient of this process, a consequence rather than a cause of

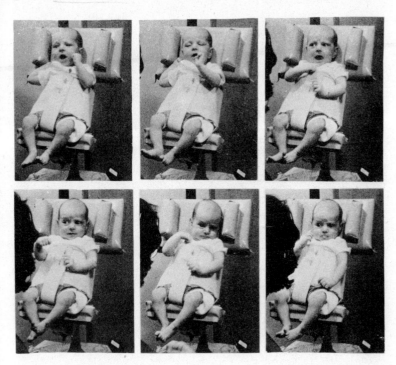

Figure 3   Babies respond to people by making many signals that show they distinguish people and that they are innately prepared to signal their intentions and interests to them. Two highly significant signals related to very complex communication activities that adults use automatically at a much higher level of differentiation are pre-speech and infant gesticulation. The smile is a vital expression of pleasure in recognition of people, but it is only one part of a complex of communication activity demonstrating the innateness of 'socialis-ing' in man. This is a baby girl only six weeks old.

understanding between persons. This position is the same as that of the Scottish philosopher John Macmurray, whose writings on the field of the personal we have found extremely stimulating.

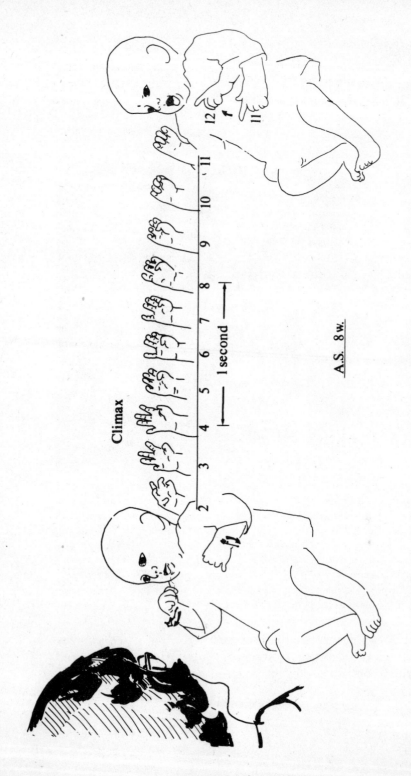

Figure 4 Prespeech movements of lips and tongue are different from those the same infants make to explore with mouth and tongue; the movements are combined in subtle gradients of 'body language' including ritualised hand-

Of course, infant communication needs a partner. It depends on a number of special adaptations in the mother's behaviour. Some of these, we find, are almost automatically fulfilled by the normal rhythm and organisation of her voluntary action, others require unconscious alterations in the way the mother would normally communicate. She behaves differently from the way she would to another adult person (Figure 5). Changes that all unaffected mothers make to slower, more emphatic but gentle movements and to 'baby talk' may come from a return of the mother to more elementary or basic components in her innate repertoire of social acts. It is certain that what she does to guide and sustain the sociable mood of the infant is natural and unconscious even though it benefits from experience with infants. Incidentally, we find no support for the fears of some psychologists that baby talk—treating a baby as a baby—may retard its learning to be a person, or to talk.

Our charts of the conversation-like exchanges between mother and infant reveal surprisingly regular patterns in time. By plotting the shift of the two partners up and down a few grades or levels of social animation we find that it is possible to show in a diagram the changing roles of mother and infant (Figure 6). Rudolph Schaffer has described how reciprocal acts of expression are established (see Chapter 4). That the mother provides needed stimuli in right measure is clear. She does stimulate, encourage, lead; but young infants do not usually take time to mimic their partners—they just play their part when the right moment comes. We feel the regulation is a mutual adjustment and that much of the periodicity in exchange originates from the infant.

The question of the role of imitation is a most important one. Our findings call into question the most widely held theory of its place in psychological and social development. This theory is usually a considerable simplification of the conclusions of psychologists who have actually studied imitation in infants. That young babies will sometimes imitate acts of others appropriately, even when to do so they must move a part of their body they cannot see, has for a long time struck

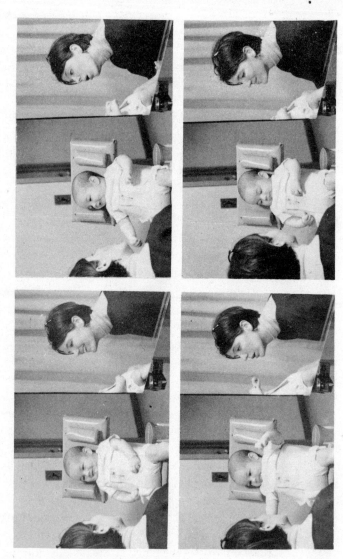

Figure 5 Films of a mother and her nine-week-old baby boy, taken with a mirror so the face expressions and movements of both can be observed from near front view, show up the patterning of early 'conversation'. The infant contributes the basic structure. The close correspondence of attitude and expression of excitement, feeling, and interest result from the mother imitating the infant, not the other way round.

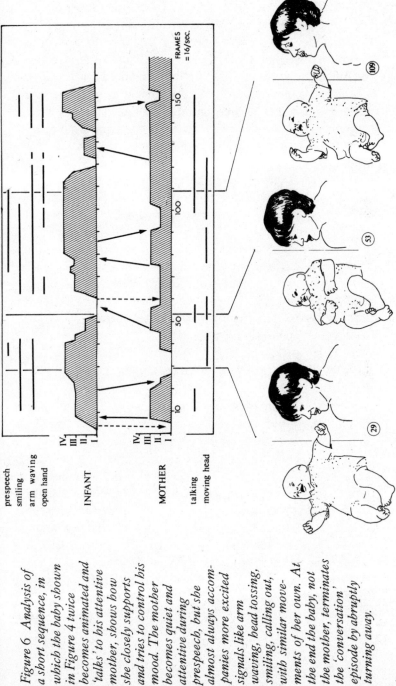

Figure 6 Analysis of a short sequence, in which the baby shown in Figure 4 twice becomes animated and 'talks' to his attentive mother, shows how she closely supports and tries to control his mood. The mother becomes quiet and attentive during prespeech, but she almost always accompanies more excited signals like arm waving, head tossing, smiling, calling out, with similar movements of her own. At the end the baby, not the mother, terminates the 'conversation' episode by abruptly turning away.

psychologists as mysterious and important. It seems to indicate
that babies learn to be persons, but any imitation also needs
an elaborate innate machinery. Even in the first month a
baby may imitate a mouth movement of the mother, or protru-
sion of her tongue. To do so the baby must have a model of
the mother's face in his brain, and this model must be properly
mapped onto the motor apparatus of his own face. Movements
of head and hands, as well as face, may elicit imitation. The
baby must have identifying models for these parts as well.

In our films of the earliest conversation, we have rarely seen
imitation of this kind in babies under six months of age, and
when it does occur the infant attends as if abstracted from the
conversational flow and intently regards what the 'instructor'
does for some time before acting to imitate. Moreover, the
partner must try to get imitation by pointedly repeating an act
in a teacher-like way that is not a common behaviour of a
mother to a young infant. On the other hand, we are impressed
with the elaborate and faithful mimicry of the more animated
acts of the baby by the mother (Figure 5). Apparently *her*
imitation is an important part of the normal encouragement
to conversational activity by the baby.

Psychological communication and the origin of language

Discovery of embryonic speaking in the social animation of
infants, nearly two years before they use words to communicate, reinforces the view of psycholinguists nowadays that
language is embedded in an innate context of non-verbal
communication by which intention and experience are transmitted from person to person. We speak with obvious purpose
to inform, instruct, direct or in some other way influence the
actions and experience of others. The meanings of single
words depend on their position in such speech acts. Infants a
few months old make speech-like patterns of movement when
they are also clearly overcome by some rudimentary purpose
to influence, impress, or lead the attentions they have obtained
of another. Even though no meaningful information about

the world is transmitted, the act is clearly one of psychological communication that may be said to show 'intersubjectivity'.

Mothers 'talking with' infants about two months of age phrase their speech so as to allow the infant to take his turn and 'have his say' in prespeech. Much of the behaviour of the baby expressing excitement or impulse to act is followed closely by the mother, and indeed her skill and understanding of what the infant is doing enable her often to obtain synchrony of emphatic acts so the two behave in complete concert as if dancing together. But this doubling of behaviour does not apply to prespeech, which is normally watched politely by the mother with little sign of imitation or shadowing. We therefore distinguish concerted joint expression of social animation from exchanged or alternated messages. It is the latter, which remind one of the interplaying melodies of music, which are potentially important for the development of conversational exchange of information about individual experiences in speech.

The use of speech to name and talk about experiences in the common field of things, people, one's actions, or the actions of others, comes, of course, much later in life, after a considerable development of exploratory and manipulative intelligence, and when free locomotion is beginning. Jean Piaget concludes that this proves the primacy of the development of schemata to know objects. It may, as Joanna Ryan of Cambridge proposes, indicate the need for considerable development of intersubjective communication without words, before words can be used to signify and specify.

The early appearance of communication with persons in the psychology of infants seems to provide what is needed for sharing all kinds of action and purpose with adults as more capable, more intelligent beings. At first infants seem fully occupied with the formalities of the interpersonal play, which we call primary or diadic intersubjectivity. But, after four months, developments in attention and object recognition, and particularly the development of controlled voluntary reaching for and manipulating and mouthing objects, mean that a conversation can become about what the infant has looked at, reached to, done. This is the beginning of games with things, or 'toys'.

Preparing the way through play

Marilyn Elliott has begun a study with me of the relationship of play in infancy to intersubjectivity. We believe that all play, in addition to the perceptual or cognitive factors discussed by Jerome Bruner (see Chapter 6), has an interpersonal element, although this may be disguised in private games when the self plays with itself. Peter Wolff of Boston has studied the earlier purely social play a mother can have in peek-a-boo or pat-a-cake with infants as young as six or eight weeks. This communication prepares the way for play with things.

If an infant of four months or so reacts to the attentions of an adult by looking pointedly at or deliberately reaching for or pointing to something, this thing becomes at once the centre of interest of the partner too. Around five months many of the infants we have studied have exhibited a marked increase in such deliberate bringing of a topic from the outside into a 'conversation'. They seem to do so more with highly familiar partners, such as their mother, than with mere friends who, unlike strangers who threaten at this age, may be treated with undivided 'conversation'.

This is the age at which it is first possible to show a baby something one is doing, and it is also the age at which strong attention to the mouth of the mother leads a baby to imitate some of her speaking movements. Clearly, such developments have great significance as preparation for the growth of language as communication about intentions and experiences with reference to people, places and things.

If we are right in the conclusion that intersubjectivity plays the key role in fostering exploration of the world, even in earliest infancy, then attachment of infants to persons is fundamentally a seeking of companionship in experience. Attachment is to a companion rather than to a caretaker. Many studies have sought to trace recognition of the mother as a particular person, or as an object with an identity; or conversely, to find when babies will show fear of strangers. Most of these record a critical change at about four or five months, and at present psychologists usually attribute this to an advance in learning powers or cognitive processes of the infant that enables better perceptual discrimination of strangers and friends. Psychoanalysts insist that this change is also a development of the affectional process—that love of the familiar caretaker is involved.

We have seen that at this same age infants frequently do not wish to play at conversation with their mothers, but will still do so with less familiar friends. Our evidence suggests that there is a relationship between a new wilfulness in social behaviour and the emerging intentions to take hold of and manipulate things. Entirely new levels of memory and perception process develop along with the appearance of effective actions on objects, and these advances are coupled to equally significant changes in the kind of dependency the infant has on the actions of others, especially those people for whom a special attachment is forming.

This interpretation agrees with the well-known findings of Harry Harlow in his experiments in the early 1960s with young monkeys who develop attachments to an artificial mother made of cloth. In exploration tests the surrogate mother clearly serves the young monkey as a pole of assurance for play with objects in a room. Subsequently, Mary Ainsworth has shown how older infants explore a strange room or make contact with strange persons more readily when with someone to whom they have developed a strong attachment. Evidently *confidence* in an infant over four or five months of age, like that of children and adults too, combines the two meanings of the word—assurance about what one is doing and intimacy with a person who shares.

A basic innateness of personal reactions in man is shown not only by the timetable of growth of functions common to all normal babies, but also in individual differences. Adults differ in personality and they behave in widely different ways with infants, some being shy and fearful of even a manifestly friendly baby; and fathers differ in important ways from mothers. We have some evidence that some fathers play a more boisterous kind of game with more jokes and mimicry of prespeech grimaces and more poking of the body than do mothers. They thereby excite infants more to calling and laughter, and to vigorous body movements. It has been found that fathers treat infant girls with more talking and gentle touching than boys with whom they are more peremptory and sometimes very vigorous. But even very young boys and girls act differently, too, showing that such sex differences are not entirely due to learning of social roles. Male babies only two months old generally have more vigorous body movements and adopt more readily a leading place in a conversational exchange with their mothers (Figure 5). Female babies tend rather to watch and follow and to act in animated face and mouth displays with fine hand gesticulation (Figure 3).

It seems very likely, from our few case studies of individual parents with infants, that there are also large inherent personality differences between adults or babies of one sex that affect the pattern of intersubjective behaviour. We need to do much more work to describe types of personality in very young persons.

Emotion in personal relations

One recent outcome of our work on intersubjectivity in early infancy throws light on the relationship between emotion and the acts that infants address to persons, a topic which is of central importance in Freudian theory of infant development. An undergraduate student, John Tatam, has performed an experiment in my laboratory on the emotional effects on an infant when a mother acts irrelevantly. He arranged, with a partial reflecting mirror and changing lights, for the mother, while remaining visible to the baby as before, to cease seeing the baby and to see an adult in the same place. The person silently asked the mother questions by holding up cards with writing on them. The infant could see only the mother. In replying at length the mother automatically changed her style of talking to that appropriate for an adult from that proper for her baby, and of course, also stopped reacting to what the infant did.

In every case the eight- to ten-week-old infants were clearly puzzled by the change in their mother, and they made exaggerated solicitations as if to get her attention back. Some quickly became dejected-looking and withdrawn, a state of acute depression which took minutes to abate when the mother's attention returned to the infant with a change in lighting.

We have since repeated the experiment with simpler procedures. If a partner conversing with a two-month-old intentionally withholds all responses and without acting in any threatening way just makes a blank face, the same transformation of the state of the baby to puzzlement and then depression is invariably observed. There remain to be investigated many different ways of disturbing the normal flow of reciprocal interpersonal activity between adult and infant to find the range of expectations of the infant, but we have established that there is a strong innate relationship of emotion to the perception of how persons respond.

John Bowlby of the Tavistock Institute of Human Relations, London, has collected abundant evidence since the last European war of the depressing effects of departure or loss of a mother, or other principle companion, on the health and spirits of babies and children. He believes initial attachments are innate, but based on a few social release mechanisms like those studied in animals by Konrad Lorenz and Harry Harlow. As Michael Rutter has explained (see Chapter 1), recent work extends the concept of attachment considerably. Tatam's experiment shows how complex is the relationship between perception of a person and emotion while a very young baby is actually communicating with someone. Obviously the basis of interpersonal relationships is highly complex and emotional from very soon after birth.

Social or socialised?

Our findings lead us to question accepted views of the socialisation of human intelligence. Jean Piaget, who believes in a strong, developing biological determination of the human

mind, conceives of infants as initially ùnaware of the separate-
ness of themselves from the world they experience. Out of
this union with experience they 'objectify' both things and
persons without distinguishing these two. He has said, however, that *following* the development of the brain schema for
an object, 'objects are conceived by analogy with the self as
active, alive and conscious', and that 'this is particularly so
with those exceptionally unpredictable and interesting objects
—people'. Our position is closer to that of Henri Wallon
regarding the early role of innate social abilities, than it is to
that of Piaget. Piaget thinks that in the first few months there
are no signs that infants respond particularly to persons as
such except reflexly, and that infant emotions are determined
by affective reflexes triggered by simple losses or gains of
equilibrium. Like Freud he attributes the foundations of human
social experience to the biological needs of the self.

Freud thought these needs were derived from feelings of
the body important for physiological maintenance, but also
gave great importance to the development of affectional functions that define an 'object relation' with the mother early in
the first year of life. As we have said, John Bowlby, who is a
psychiatrist and psychoanalyst, accepts the ethologists' idea
of attachment through innate releasers in adult and baby, and
imprinting of the baby to a particular person who is usually
the mother.

Rudolph Schaffer of Strathclyde University, Glasgow, says
'An infant is essentially an asocial being,' that 'other people,
he soon finds out, are fascinating things to watch, feel and
listen to, but as yet they do not constitute a class of stimuli
distinct from the inanimate world' and that 'children are not
born "knowing" people'. (see Chapter 4.)

But our films show that infants *are* adapted, at the latest
by three weeks after birth, to approach persons and objects
as if they are quite different. The elaborateness of social
responses and social expressions in the second and third months
of life, before an infant has begun deliberate and controlled
handling and mouthing of objects, indicates that intersubjec-

tivity is fitted into development from the start as a determining influence. Human social intelligence is the result of development of an innate human mode of psychological function that requires transactions with other persons. This function includes rudiments of the quite unique human activity of speech, which becomes the chief medium of individual human mental growth and the essential ingredient of civilised society.

Interaction of praxis (doing) and communication

I believe that the evolution of experimental or scientific thought processes in the mind of a child, and the object-perception processes associated with them, may at times develop in competition or disequilibrium with the growth of intersubjectivity with persons. But I also feel certain that the normal development of cognitive mastery of the world is one that advances through cooperative interaction of private experiment and social communication. Neither is sufficient alone for psychological development to occur.

Humans project their minds into the world to invest objects and events with intention, not because they confuse themselves with the world, but because they have such a fundamental gift for communication with the intentions of persons that mirror themselves and that they mirror in reply. That such animate abilities are biologically founded in man suggests that they have a determining role in the plan of growth and the changes in the life of individuals. I believe this concept of a growing innate social function will prove necessary to understand the cooperative efforts of humans of different ages in families, in schools, in business, in sport—anywhere where people create mutual activity.

At this point neurobiological considerations which encouraged my initial enquiry into infancy have receded far into the distance. Now I am involved in psychobiological considerations for which known anatomical schemes are unhelpful. Specialised nerve networks in orderly arrays must be there, but I have not the remotest notion of how or where they may be specified in the brain. This is an important caution. The day is far distant when psychology can look for anatomical explanations of its more complex functions. The mechanisms of psychological action will remain largely imaginary. In spite of this, descriptive research shows strongly formed innate foundations of psychological processes, including orderly changes of personality in the life of each growing individual.

Speech makes babies move
WILLIAM CONDON

An observer watching people communicate is confronted by the seemingly continuous and ongoing nature of their behaviour. When someone talks, for example, his whole body appears to accompany his voice; his head moves this way and that, he gesticulates with his arms, and he shifts in his chair. The listener is also often moving in various ways while the speaker is talking. The listener may, for instance, be reaching for and lighting a cigarette or toying with the matches. How can the observer discover the segments or 'pieces' of which these organised individual and interactional behaviours are composed? This is a constant problem facing an investigator trying to understand human communication. One approach has been to take pictures and sound films of human interaction and study them frame by frame in the search for 'Units' and other patterns. This approach might best be called the linguistic-kinesic (body motion) analysis of behaviour. (It has sometimes been inaccurately referred to as non-verbal communication.) There are many sub-areas within this broad field. I should like to focus on neonate-caretaker communication, particularly my recent hypothesis, developed with Dr Louis Sander, that the neonate moves synchronously with adult speech as early as the first day after birth.

Such an hypothesis suggests the implication that humans are not as isolated from each other as they thought and it supports the notion that language acquisition may be prepared for by nature (innate). The phrase 'moves synchronously with adult speech' requires some background explanation, since such neonate synchronisation is part of a wider process of human synchronisation. In terms of the present focus the question becomes: What are the observable 'units' and their boundaries such that it can be specified that units of the body motion of the neonate occur in an ordered relationship to the units of adult speech?

Analysis of filmed movements

I have spent more than a decade in the micro-analysis of the organisation of human behaviour and communication using sound films. This involved observing a sound film repeatedly until pattern and order began to emerge in the behaviour. The universe being observed was permitted to reveal the structure within it, rather than 'units' being projected into it in an *a priori* fashion. Initially, I spent several months studying the films from a relatively macroscopic perspective. I observed closely gestures and their related lexical contexts, but, although it was interesting, it was not productive. There were always body motion changes discernible below this gestural level which remained unaccounted for in terms of their relationship to the total behaviour. What was lacking was a set of trust-worthy 'units' based on a rigorous analysis of the behaviour itself.

To try to circumvent these problems I carried out an analysis which systematically followed the structure of movement change down to more and more minute levels, finally reaching a point where I could detect no smaller changes of movement using film running at 24 and 48 frames per second. I then spent several years at this very micro level in a reverse process of systematically analysing the structure of the organisation of behaviour (with the emphasis on organisation) back up to the more macroscopic level of one second and above. It took a number of years to clarify the complex, interlocking 'levels' of behavioural organisation occurring within the duration of even one second. At least five integrated levels of linguistic-kinesic organisation occur within that short span of time. That is about the amount of time it takes to emit a four- or five-word phrase. I discovered that a unified organisation existed between speech and body motion across all these levels in normal speaker behaviour.

This intensive, micro analysis led to the observation and description of 'Minimal units' of behaviour which still remain forms of organisation. They are distinguishable as forms of order with describable boundaries, and while this gives them a certain discrete quality, they remain forms of pattern within the total ongoing organisations of the behaviour. With respect to the development of the main theme of this article I need first to describe the nature of these 'units' of human behaviour and the method of their derivation. This requires careful explanation of how that behaviour is organised.

The relationship between the behaviour of the listener and the speaker can be examined in terms of such basic 'units', which in turn must be described prior to dealing with the behaviour of the neonate in response to adult speech. As previously indicated, when a person speaks there are usually several body parts moving together simultaneously. These co-occurring and overlapping movements posed a difficult problem for segmentation until a primary *form-of-order* was observed to be characteristic of the movement of these body parts in relation to each other and to speech. Movement could not be reduced to discrete body-part movements, of which it could then be said to be composed, because several parts were almost always moving simultaneously. However, I discovered a form of order that was being sustained between these simultaneously moving parts for brief durations. These brief durations (lasting up to one sixth of a second) of coordinated behaviour movements can be called behaviour quanta. I gave these behavioural quanta the name 'process units' to emphasise their organisational nature in contrast to a discrete or atomistic view. These process units are features within wider organised processes, forming a self-synchronous rhythm-hierarchy which seems to be characteristic of human speaker behaviour. This rhythm-hierarchy is the integrated product of patterns discernible within the ongoing processing of behaviour. The view I am presenting, then, is that of a unified organism having intricate and self-synchronous behaviour which is analysable (but not separable) into integrated sub-organisations or forms of order.

Analysis of movement

The observation and empirical description of these minimal units, and the wider rhythm-hierarchy in which they participate, provide a 'microscope' for the analysis of the organisation of both normal and pathological behaviour. The equipment and method I used allowed me to study sustained movements and the points of change of direction of movement of each part of the body of the people in the film, including eyes, brows, and mouth, down to the level of one film frame. The body joints with their characteristic modes of extension-flexion, pronation-supination, and adduction-abduction, constitute the primary descriptive categories. All body parts which can be detected moving (from head to feet) are carefully analysed, with a notation made for each part, using lines for frames during which movement in a given direction is sustained and arrows at the frame where change in direction or speed of movement occurs. I was also able to compare speech and body motion 'events' and to analyse the possible forms of order in their relationships.

The 'process unit' emerged from observing human behaviour using these techniques. This is the postulated, minimal form of organisation of behaviour, defined by the order in the relationships of several body parts sustaining movement together. While these several body parts may move in different directions and with differing speeds, they will sustain those speeds and movements together in relationship to each other as a sort of 'moving, configurational unity' for a brief duration. Sustaining the relationship for that brief time results in a sort of behavioural 'mode' or entity in contrast to preceding and following entities similarly sustained. This is a difficult concept to articulate verbally although it is easily grasped when illustrated visually with film. Figure 1 illustrates such process units.

Behaviour is composed of the serial emergence of such 'bundles' which are in turn organised into wider dimensions. Thus as a person speaks his body moves as an integrated totality in harmony with the emergent speech. This hierarchic, rhythmic organisation of speech and body motion appears to be a manifestation or function of more basic behavioural rhythms. Figure 2 presents a tentative schema of the rhythm-hierarchy.

Behaviour in 'process units' or quanta at the minimal level may be characteristic of nervous systems in general. Behaviour

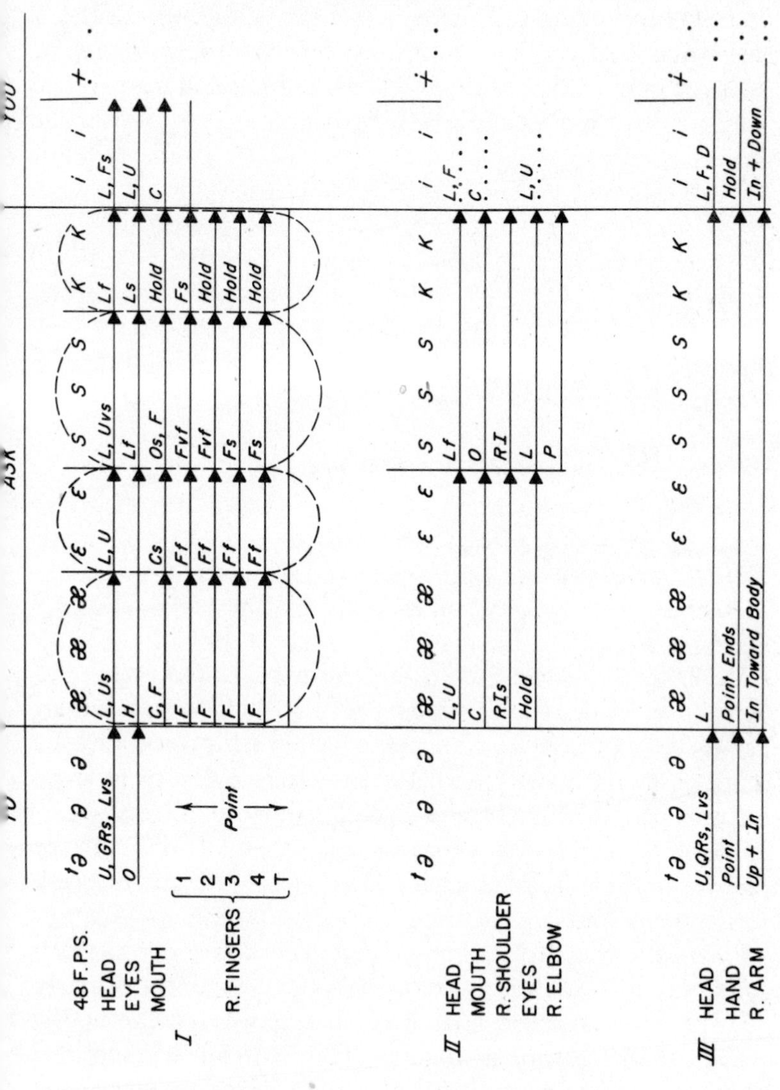

Figure 1 'Process Units' and the synchronisation of body motion with the hierarchic, articulatory structuring of the word 'ask'. 'Ask' is analysable into the four encircled linguistic-kinesic quanta. The body also accompanies the syllabic (ae ae ae ee) and (sss kk) level as well as the word as an entirety.

TO   ASK   YOU

I
- 48 F.P.S.
- HEAD
- EYES
- MOUTH
- R.FINGERS { 1 2 3 4 T }

II
- HEAD
- MOUTH
- R.SHOULDER
- EYES
- R.ELBOW

III
- HEAD
- HAND
- R.ARM

is essentially organised. When a ball player throws a ball his behaviour is skilfully organised. As he draws back to throw, his eyes must be on the batter and as he throws all the parts of his body are organisationally involved in the delivery of the ball.

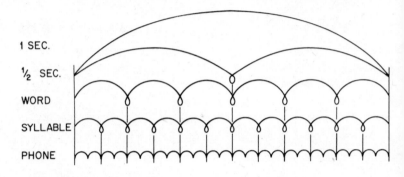

Figure 2   Illustrative schema of the rhythm hierarchy. The phone, syllable and word levels would represent, for example, the organisation presented in the word 'ask' in Figure 1.

He pitches as a total, unified organism. As a lion walks, his legs move in organised, ongoing relationships to each other. That behaviour occurs in these self-synchronous, quantal bundles at the most minimally detectable level (using these techniques) is the most basic observation of micro-kinesis. This offers an important basis for the analysis of disorganised behaviour since these quantal forms were observed to break up in many forms of pathology.

The movement of a listener also occurs in terms of such process units. Continued micro-analysis led me to the startling observation, however, that a listener moves synchronously with a speaker during interaction. This is usually a completely 'unconscious' reaction. It seems to be a form of precise and almost simultaneous entrainment on the part of the listener in relation to the emergent articulatory patterning of the speaker's speech. It thus offers a precise assessment of responsivity to sound. The composition of a listener's 'process units' usually differs from those of a speaker. The listener, for example, may be moving his legs and fingers while the speaker may move his arms and head. There is an ongoing isomorphism or entrainment between the listener's process units and the speaker's speech. It is like an intricate and subtle dance which is always occurring during interactions. This has been called interactional synchrony and is also 'hierarchic' in nature like self-synchrony. There is tentative evidence to suggest that the more people share movement and/or posture together the greater their rapport during those moments. Moving together seems to indicate greater rapport than posture sharing, however. Communication thus seems to simultaneously and necessarily contain such things as talking about the weather and other daily events and also, at the moment these things are being discussed, 'statements' concerning the relationships between the talkers, usually unconscious. The point to be made is that human beings seem to be much more participants together within a wider communicational matrix, which has biological foundations, than they are isolated entities sending messages. Figure 3 illustrates interactional synchrony.

The observation of such interactional synchronisation led me to wonder how early in life it might begin. To answer this question I joined with Dr Louis Sander in a project designed to study neonate response to human speech. We videotaped eleven normal neonates (with sound film subsequently made from the tape) and five normal neonates directly sound-filmed. Fourteen of these infants were from twelve hours to two days old, and the other two were two weeks old. We used an audio tape containing American English, isolated vowel sounds, tapping sounds, and Chinese language excerpts as stimuli, as well as a living adult speaker. We observed that infants moved in precise synchrony with the articulatory structure of adult speech. Such synchrony was often precisely sustained by an infant across long sequences of words. Figure 4 illustrates this synchronisation.

First hours after birth

It appears, then, that interactional synchrony begins as early as the first few hours after birth and may exist even earlier. If the infant, from the beginning, moves in such precise, shared

88 William Condon

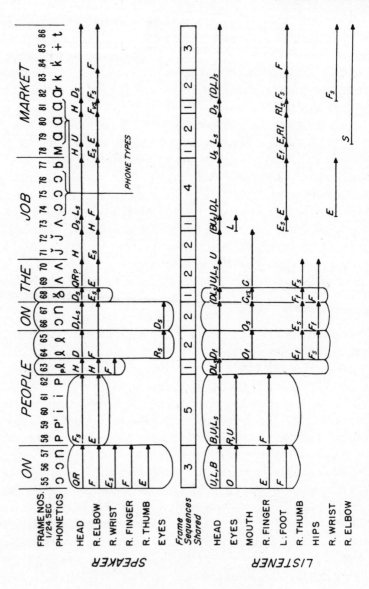

Figure 3 Interactional synchrony: the phrase 'on people on the job market' is taken from a much longer sequence during a conversation between two adult males. The listener's body (bottom) is moving in process units or quanta which are of the same form as those of the speaker.

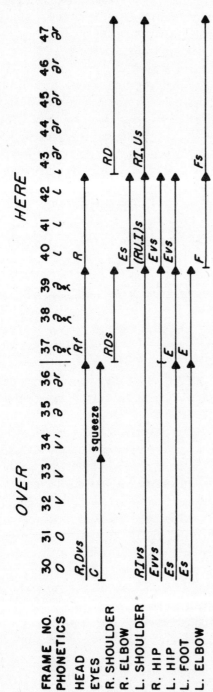

Figure 4 Infant synchronisation with adult speech: this segment is taken from an eighty-nine word sequence spoken to a two-day-old child by a male doctor. The baby's body moves in synchrony with the speech.

rhythm with the organisation of the speech structure of his culture, then he participates developmentally (through complex sociobiological entrainment processes) in literally millions of repetitions of linguistic forms long before he will use them in speaking and communicating. By the time he begins to speak he may have already laid down within himself the form and structure of the language system of his culture. This would encompass a multiplicity of interlocking aspects; rhythmic and syntactic 'hierarchies', pitch and stress patterns, paralinguistic nuances, not to mention body motion styles and rhythms. This may prove an empirical basis for a new approach to language acquisition and enculturation.

The ability to examine the micro-organisational behaviour of both infants and adults and the nature of their response to sound at fractions of a second, provides a 'microscope' for the detection and analysis of abnormalities. Most clinicians use an implicit model of gross normal coordination when judging a lack of coordination. These sound-film, micro-analytic techniques are providing a method for the precise analysis of the developmental organisation of normal infant behaviour. It has also been possible to observe marked motor asynchronies in a two-week-old, at-risk infant which had been anoxic for seven minutes at birth. These asynchronies were not, however, detectable clinically.

In summary, a new perspective on the micro-organisation of human behaviour and communication is beginning to emerge. It reveals normal behaviour as remarkably self-synchronous. More important, however, it has revealed a precise, ongoing communicational synchronisation between the body movements of a listener and the articulatory structure of a speaker's speech. Our studies suggest that such synchronisation begins as early as the day of birth. The hypothesis thus implies that the neonate participates immediately and deeply in communication and is not an isolate which slowly develops such skills after many months. If this is indeed the case, it may require a reconceptualisation of infant capacities, particularly the impact of the early environment in relation to such sensitivity.

The development of language
JOANNA RYAN

Before 1960 psychological work on language development
had been sporadic, and all the main theories of child development, whether psychoanalytic, cognitive (Piagetian) or behaviourist, had largely ignored it. The sources of the current
revival of interest in language development lie largely outside
psychology, in linguistics, in communications theory, and
in compensatory education. Only now is psychology beginning
to formulate its own theories about how adults deal with the
complexities of language—the sounds, the grammar, the meaning of words and sentences—at the level of individual processing.
It has barely made a start on how we talk to each other in mutual
dialogues, speaking appropriately and in turn, combining
linguistic with non-linguistic forms of communication. We
now know something about how children master the more
formal aspects of language, particularly the grammar (see
Cromer, Chapter 10). We know only a little about how such
skills grow out of social interaction with others, and how these
skills are used to further this interaction.

Most children learn to speak and understand their native
language without any deliberate and institutionalised instruction of the kind needed to read and write. One of the main
psychological concerns has been with how this happens, with
whether the processes involved can be regarded as forms of
learning, and if so, of what kind. Psychologists have also done
a lot of descriptive work distinguishing various 'stages' of
language development and establishing age norms for these
stages amongst European and American children. Such information is useful for assessing and diagnosing the more
serious language disorders. In addition, some important differences between groups of children with respect to the rate
of language development have been found using these
measures. For example, girls tend to be ahead of boys from

infancy to early puberty, when the differences disappear; children from middle-class homes tend to be ahead of those from working-class homes from about the second year of life, with the differences increasing with age; and first-born children tend to be ahead of later-born ones. However, the measures used are very crude and their use in this way presents an over-homogenised view of language development. The discreteness of the stages is questionable and for many children the stages are not easily identifiable.

Psychologists who take a stage approach to language development also tend to emphasise its maturational and biological basis, with increasing brain maturation and specialisation as a major determinant of the pace and course of language development. However, even if we knew more than we do about the details of early brain development, there still remains the problem of evaluating its causal role. Much of the evidence is correlational, and except in some pathological cases, neurological processes can never be regarded as sufficient explanations. An example of such ambiguity is seen in the interpretation of the sex difference in language development mentioned above. Can the girls' faster development be associated with earlier maturation of the brain structures involved in speech functions? (see Lloyd and Archer, Chapter 16, and Hutt, Chapter 15).

The problem here is that the main neurological evidence concerns lateralisation of the brain (into left and right hemisphere functions, speech usually being on the left). This process occurs earlier in girls than in boys, but only around the age of four or five, by which time both have been speaking and understanding for several years. The differential maturation of earlier neurological processes related to speech is mostly supposition at the moment. However, we also know that parents, particularly mothers, behave differently towards infants depending on sex, in ways that are relevant to language. For example, mothers are more likely to respond to girls in the first year of life by talking to them than they are to boys, whom they are more likely to touch. Girl babies also tend to be more socially responsive than boys, and this may well be an important precursor to early communication skills. None of these suggestions are incompatible with each other, and none of them could be sufficient explanations on their own. Further, there is no reason to suppose that the relative importance of any one factor is fixed and the same in all children.

Chaotic speech

A minimal role has, however, been assigned to the environment, in the sense of the speech a child hears around him, by Noam Chomsky and some of his psychologist followers. One of their main arguments is that the formal structure of language is so complex that no child could in principle learn the correct production and understanding of various grammatical forms that is in fact observed in young children. The fragmentary, chaotic and often incorrect nature of much of adult speech is cited as providing insufficient learning material, and as showing the magnitude of the task before the child. This assumption about adult speech has in fact turned out to be incorrect, since, as will become apparent, much of it is very finely adjusted to children's capabilities.

Chomsky was led by these and other considerations to postulate the existence of innate equipment with which all children are born, this equipment consisting in some of the supposedly universal features of all language, and allowing the child to abstract the particular rules of his or her native language. A fruitless polarisation has taken place around these issues, reaching its depths in the much publicised dog-fight between Chomsky and B. F. Skinner, and in an attack by Chomsky's supporters on a psychologist (Martin Braine at Washington University) for ignoring the abstract structure of language in his explanation of early language development.

Meanwhile . . . back in the nursery—or at least in the white middle-class nursery—many fascinating details have been discovered about the course of language development, stimulated by Chomskian linguistics of the period. For example, Roger Brown and his associates at Harvard have shown how the final full use of some grammatical rules builds up gradually by the addition of various component rules, starting from the initial primitive forms. For example, the correct use of interrogatives such as 'Where is she going?' and 'What is that?' only occurs after intermediate forms such as 'Where she go?' and 'What that is?' have been used. Even earlier forms of questions consist in phrases such as 'What that?' used routinely in many situations with no substitution of more appropriate items, such as 'where' or 'this'.

Intricate grammars have now been written for many aspects of developing speech. At this level of detail relatively little conformity is found between children as regards either the types or the precise succession of rules needed to describe their speech, to the extent that some children appear to be completely idiosyncratic. However, one general point of some importance has emerged from such work, namely that children's attempts at speech are not just simple and erroneous derivatives of adult speech. Instead much of children's speech has its own rules and regularities and contains forms which are not found in adult speech, and which, therefore, cannot have been copied. A common example is the production of forms such as 'I goed', and 'foots' (see Cromer, Chapter 10). Such systematic over-generalisation to exceptional cases happens even where the child has previously used the irregular form correctly before acquiring the more general rule. Similarly, when children first combine two or more words together they sometimes use combinations that it is most unlikely adults will have used.

The data on which much of the Harvard work was based was collected from only three children. They were tape-recorded at home with other family members at regular intervals over a long period, with no experimental manipulation other than the presence of the observer and his tape-recorder. Individual case studies of this kind, often of the writer's own child, have a long tradition in this area, as does naturalistic observation, and most of the ideas have come from these sources. It may surprise readers that so much weight is put on such limited numbers, and on such sampling methods. Similar studies urgently need extending to other social classes, cultures and languages. Individual case studies will, however, remain an important source of information, aided now by video recording. They are essential for the analysis of the fine details of everyday interaction that constitute a child's life, and also for describing how one child differs from another, and how these differences can be related to differences in the child's environment. Studies of this detail that chart developmental changes are extremely time-consuming to carry out: one hour of audio and video recording may take 10 hours to transcribe accurately, and another 10 to analyse.

Until recently most work has concentrated on the child's grasp of phonology, grammar and vocabulary. Just as important as these skills are social skills which allow a child to carry on a mutual dialogue with others, to speak in turn and appropriately to what is being said or happening. Much of children's earliest speech does not have this other-directed quality. It often takes the form of an erratic monologue, not apparently requiring any reciprocation or else directed at animals or toys. Young children often do not reply when spoken to, and often imitate questions rather than answer them. They sometimes repeat their own utterances in quick succession, often changing the sounds as if playing with the words.

Interpreting speech

Another phenomenon that shows how much has to be learned about the communicative as opposed to the formal aspects of speech, is that a child may say something that is intelligible standard English and yet we may not understand what he is trying to say, why he has said it. Such ambiguity is particularly likely with single-word utterances. A child may say 'Cat' and this can be interpreted as a comment on the cat's presence or on its disappearance, as a request for the cat, or for its removal, and so on. Clues to interpretation will include the circumstances of the utterance, the child's intonation and other behaviour at the time.

Psychologists have also noticed that mothers often repeat what their child has just said, and at the same time add something to it. For example, if the child says 'Cat milk', the mother may reply, 'Mm, the cat's drinking her milk,' or 'No, the cat can't have your milk.' Such a process was called expansion by Roger Brown who first noticed it, and it appears to be a special but common feature of adult-child interaction. Expansion is an automatic process—most adults are unaware of themselves doing it, and find it impossible to stop when it is pointed out. One of its functions may be to allow the mother to check that she has interpreted the child correctly, by specifying the meaning of the child's ambiguous utterance more precisely than the child was able to do. For the child, expansions may provide a rich source of grammatical and contextual information, related very immediately to what he or she has just said. They also tell the child what he or she has been taken to mean.

There are many other ways in which adult-child interaction differs from adult-adult interaction. It has been found that mothers' speech to children is slower, simpler in many respects, and also grammatically more correct than is their speech to adults, and that the extent of this alteration depends on the age and capabilities of the child. The effective linguistic environment for the child is thus more helpful than has been assumed. It is also found that a very high proportion of mothers' speech to children takes the form of questions, even before the child is capable of answering verbally. Such questioning may be a forceful means of drawing a child into a dialogue, a way of eliciting attention and establishing mutual orientation between the mother and child, rather than a request for information or for confirmation.

Whilst adults repeat and add something to the utterances of children, children frequently repeat and delete something from the utterances of adults. Just as adults vary in the extent to which they expand their children's utterances, so children vary in the extent to which they imitate, some children not imitating at all. Behaviourist psychologists have elevated imitation into the major mechanism of learning to talk, but they are then faced with explaining how children who don't imitate learn language. Other psychologists, particularly those influenced by Chomsky, have proclaimed imitation to be of no relevance to the learning of grammar, on the grounds that mastery of a language does not consist in the ability to produce memorised sentences, but rather in the flexible application of rules to produce and understand indefinitely many new sentences.

Recent work, however, has shown that imitation can be a source of both new vocabulary and new grammatical forms. The children who do imitate tend to imitate items that they do not use spontaneously, but which are not entirely strange to them. Thus, many items and rules are only used spontaneously after they have first been used imitatively. Children have also been observed to imitate their mother's expansions of their own speech and this may be a particularly useful kind of imitation. Imitation tends to decline after about the age of three. It is essential that it does disappear since it is in fact a conversational deadend—try carrying on a conversation with someone who only imitates you!

Most of this detailed descriptive work on adult-child interaction is only loosely connected to the broad theoretical approaches mentioned earlier. The field is no longer so dominated by the crudely quantitative questions about rate of development, nor by such oversimplified concepts as the 'environment' or 'maturation'. The analytic categories that are now being suggested by psychologists for describing the various processes of language development will allow us to ask much more sensible questions. Psychologists are now also turning their attention to what is known as pre-speech (see Trevarthan, Chapter 7) and to the establishment of non-vocal communication between the child and others. This will set subsequent language development in a realistic social context.

Acquisition of grammar
RICHARD CROMER

Ask parents how a child learns to speak, and they will answer with great assurance that the child imitates what he hears. Given also careful instruction by parents and teachers to avoid what is ungrammatical, the child eventually comes to possess the adult grammar of the language to which he is exposed. That, at least, is the common notion.

It is surprising how this view prevails in spite of so much evidence to the contrary in children's utterances. Can it be that three-quarters of a century of one particular psychological view of how the organism learns has filtered down into the general belief structure in our culture? The Chomskyan revolution in linguistics has severely challenged these assumptions. Whatever else modern linguists have accomplished, they have served notice on developmental psychologists that, as yet, we simply have no real understanding of how the child learns to speak his native language. We need to understand these processes if we are ever to be able to help those children who, for a variety of reasons, fail to acquire language.

In discussing the problem I will restrict myself to the grammatical aspects of language—ignoring the many interesting problems of communication in general as well as the purely phonological acquisition of speech sounds. 'Grammatical' will refer to a *description* of what speakers of a language do in fact say, rather than to the *prescriptive* or 'school-type' grammars representing someone's opinion about what people ought to say. With this in mind, we can turn to the utterances children make to see if we can learn something about how they learn to speak.

For several years, Roger Brown and his colleagues at Harvard University have recorded all the utterances made during a two hour period at home every other week by several children. Careful analyses of the 'sentences' uttered by these children (and by children in several other studies as well) confirm some of the points made by Chomsky on a more theoretical level—namely, that children do not acquire language through such methods as imitation, frequency, practice, and reinforcement (reward), as is commonly supposed. Let us examine each of these briefly. There is only space here for a few examples from the data which illustrate why these principles are inadequate by themselves to explain the language acquisition process. After this short negative review about what language acquisition is not, we can examine some new and perhaps controversial ideas concerning language learning as well as suggest several types of underlying abilities which may be necessary for any language acquisition to occur.

Infants' own language structure

The first evidence that imitation is not the process by which language is learned comes from a linguistic analysis of the utterances children make. The grammar of the child has its own rules. He does not treat adult utterances by dropping certain words and thus merely reducing their length. Rather, he produces grammatical structures which follow a specific form which can be described by writing the rules of his grammar at different ages. For example, when the child first begins to produce negative sentences, he simply places a negative morpheme ('no' or 'not') at the beginning of an affirmative utterance. Thus, he does not say 'Don't wipe my finger' or 'It doesn't fit', nor does he produce merely a reduction of these sentences. Instead, he says things like 'No wipe finger' and 'Not fit', which conform to his rules for producing negative statements.

Ursula Bellugi of Roger Brown's research group first listed a series of rules that children use developmentally over several years to produce negative sentences. She has also pointed out numerous other rules children use in producing their speech. For example, as the child organises the auxiliary verb system, he produces the complete auxiliary verb even in places where adults mainly use a contracted form. The auxiliary 'will' was found to be almost invariably contracted to ' 'll' when used in declarative sentences by the parents of the children studied. Typical adult utterances made to the child were 'I'll fix it later', 'We'll have to look', 'You'll ruin it', 'That'll be enough'. At the same time, however, the child was producing the non-contracted full form of 'will': 'I will stand on my knees', 'We will buy Becky a new one', 'I will read you book'. Indeed, parents have often noticed that their children sound in some sense more 'precise' in their speech in this way.

What the child seems to have done is to have acquired a set of related transformational structures. The parents also produce the non-contracted form of 'will', but always in questions: 'Will it be fun?', 'Will you finish it?' The child apparently analyses the declarative form as being related to the interrogative (question) form, and produces the non-contracted full form of 'will' in both. As Ursula Bellugi puts it, the child's speech bears a relationship to the adult model, but is independent of it in characteristic ways.

There are many other structures which exemplify this same type of rule-governed process. Another rather interesting case has to do with the verb 'think'. In certain meanings in English, adults mainly use a construction like 'I don't think he'll come'. This is understood to mean not that one isn't thinking, but that someone isn't coming. Yet although children hear this idiomatic form in the speech of the adults around them, they mainly use a form consistent with their own rules, and say 'I think he won't come'.

Two kinds of imitation

At the same time, it is recognised that children do mimic some of the things they hear. But we must ask whether this is the *process* by which language is acquired. Indeed, is there anything special about what utterances children do imitate? There are two kinds of imitation: spontaneous and instructed. In spontaneous imitation, the child, in his own free speech, repeats phrases which an adult has uttered a few moments before. Instructed imitation occurs when an adult tells the child to imitate his utterance.

In spontaneous imitation, it has generally been found that the child mainly imitates only those structures already appearing in his own free speech—that is, those conforming to his own rule system. He also imitates some phrases slightly in advance of his level, those he will begin spontaneously to use very shortly. Again, in instructed imitation, the child rarely imitates in advance of his spontaneous speech. Instead, he drops or distorts portions of the utterance he is asked to repeat, and makes them conform to his own rules. For example, before he is spontaneously producing auxiliary verbs, these are dropped in his imitations: 'Where did he go?' is repeated back as 'Where he go?' and 'Are you coming?' as 'You coming?' Sentences like 'Dogs don't like it' are distorted into the child's own forms and are given back as 'No dog like it'. It is difficult to get the child to break his grammatical rules. This is true not only when they are wrong from the adult point of view but also when they are correct.

I recently tested 41 five- and six-year-old children on some imitation tasks. I told each child to repeat exactly what I said no matter how silly it was. I first asked them to repeat 'The grass is green', which all the children did without difficulty. Then, to be sure they understood the task, I asked them to repeat 'Grass green the is', an utterance of the identical length using the same words, but violating normal grammatical order. And much to the embarrassment of most imitation theories, not one child was able to repeat those four words accurately. They stuttered and stumbled but could not do it. (The closest any child came was one Biblical girl who came out with 'Green grass thou art'!)

It seems that imitation itself is not a process which can account for language acquisition. Obviously, exposure to adult utterances is essential, but it may be more fruitful to think in terms of the child's rule-governed attempts to match a model more and more accurately, rather than in terms of simple imitative functions.

Learning through practice and frequency

Two other principles which are often mentioned as being crucial to language acquisition are the amount of practice the child has in uttering particular grammatical forms, and the frequency with which certain forms occur in the adult speech around him. Practice, often called the 'principle of use', is immediately contradicted by children's language data such as that mentioned earlier. For example, the child has practised certain rule-governed but non-adult constructions such as 'No wipe finger' and 'Not fit' for many months. But such 'practice' does not prevent him from changing his rule system at later stages of development.

One can consider both practice and frequency together by noting children's use of strong verbs and strong nouns. Strong verbs are those like 'run' and 'go' which have their own past tense form ('ran', 'went') rather than having '-ed' attached (as in 'started' and 'walked'). Strong nouns are nouns with their own plural form ('mouse' becomes 'mice') instead of adding some form of 's' to the singular. Both strong verbs and strong nouns are frequent in the adult speech the child hears, and they are frequently used by young children. For many months, the child will happily say 'went' and 'ran'. And then, at some point, he adopts the rule of adding '-ed' to form the past tense. When he does this he immediately begins to say 'goed' and 'runned'. In other words, when a rule system is acquired, grammatical forms which the child has heard with great frequency and which he has practised daily, are driven out by forms he has never uttered and which have occurred with zero frequency in the speech around him.

Roger Brown has made systematic counts of the use of various grammatical forms both by the children he was studying and by the parents of these children. He found that the children acquired the various grammatical forms in approximately the same order. Furthermore, the parents of the children used these forms with about the same frequency as one another. But there was no relation between the parental frequencies and the order of emergence of these forms in the children's speech.

Reinforcement

Finally, what about reinforcement? It is well known that people will increase certain types of verbal behaviour if they are reinforced for that behaviour. Psychoanalysts can get their patients to talk about certain topics merely by using positive nods when the patient happens to speak about those topics. People also copy the behaviour of others whom they see being rewarded. In one experiment, children observed a model being reinforced for using prepositional phrases. Since these children then increased their own frequency of use of prepositional phrases, the experimenters concluded that reinforcement was one of the major processes by which children acquire various language structures.

There are two considerations, however, which make one wary of such a conclusion. First, the children in the experiment already knew prepositional phrases; all that was really demonstrated was that children increased their use of a form they already possessed in their own grammar. Moreover, a second experiment by other researchers again demonstrated the importance of the child's rule system. In the second experiment, a control group was included who watched models being rewarded not for normal prepositional phrases of the form preposition-article-noun (as in the phrases 'in the box', 'on an elephant') but for a distorted form, article-noun-preposition (for example, 'the box in', 'an elephant on'). The children in this control condition also increased their use of prepositional phrases—*normal* prepositional phrases, and not the distorted ones for which they had seen the model being rewarded.

Roger Brown also searched his data for evidence of the effects of positive and negative reinforcement in the natural home situation in which his recordings of language were made. For example, a phrase was listed as being positively reinforced if the mother immediately made comments such as 'That's right', and 'Good'. He found that parents mainly reinforced utterances for their truth value and almost never for syntax. As Brown humorously put it, if reinforcement was the method by which children acquire language, we would expect the end product to be a person who is always truthful but ungrammatical. But what we often find instead is the reverse!

Innate receptivity for language

There are other learning theories, of course, which postulate different processes and mechanisms for the acquisition of new material. I have dwelt on these particular principles, however, because they are also the kinds of notions most people have about how children acquire language. If under close scrutiny they seem to be less than satisfactory as explanatory principles, then we must ask: What are the mechanisms by which the child accomplishes the extraordinary feat of acquiring the complex grammar of his native language in so short a period? Noam Chomsky has proposed that evolution has built in a readiness on the part of the human organism to acquire language—a kind of innate device specially attuned to organising and structuring heard language in particular ways. When this idea was suggested, it was met with a good deal of scepticism. Many psychologists are wary of claims made for innate mechanisms in human beings. However, in the last few years there has been an increasing acceptance of the notion of innate perceptual analysers in the visual system. And recently, experiments by Peter Eimas have shown that the perception of speech differs from the perception of nonspeech acoustic signals even in infants as young as one month of age. Thus, there is evidence of innate or at least very early language analysers. Might some of these be specifically grammatical?

I have been doing some experiments on the understanding of one particular linguistic structure by children in the hope of finding out something about how children acquire language generally. The structure is one which is usually rendered by linguists as the contrast pair 'John is eager to please' and 'John is easy to please'. In the first sentence, somehow the adult speaker of English knows that John is the actor; John does the pleasing. But in the second sentence, 'John is easy to please', we know that John is not the actor; someone else pleases John.

These sentences have what linguists call a similar 'surface structure'. This surface structure is what we hear or read. But in order to interpret sentences, we analyse them down into their 'deep structure' relationships. Thus, we know that John is not the actor in the second sentence above because we are unconsciously aware that it really comes from a deep structure we might render as 'That someone pleases John is easy', where it can be seen that 'someone' and not John is the actor. Young children do not know how to process such sentences in the adult manner. With these sentences they believe that the subject ('John') is always the actor. At some point however, they acquire the knowledge that some sentences of this type require the recovery of a different deep structure. But how does one know which deep structure to recover? The only clue to correct interpretation is in the word which is used— 'eager' or 'easy' in this example. Thus, a second kind of learning is necessary. One must learn which words point to which deep structures.

In order to study these learning processes, I gave children from five to ten years of age two hand puppets—one the head of a wolf and the other the head of a duck. They put these on their hands and were asked to show both the wolf biting the duck and the duck biting the wolf. When they were familiar with the puppets and that either animal could bite the other, they were told they were going to play a game in which they had to show which animal did the biting according to the meaning of several sentences. Here are the sentences the children were given. After each sentence, the child was asked to show which animal did the biting:

The wolf is *happy* to bite
The duck is *keen* to bite
The wolf is *tasty* to bite
The duck is *easy* to bite
The wolf is *willing* to bite
The wolf is *hard* to bite
The duck is *glad* to bite
The duck is *fun* to bite

On this task, the youngest children, about five or six years old, always thought that the named animal did the biting. That this interpretation was specific to this structure was demonstrated when they were quite willing to show the non-named animal as doing the biting when given passive sentences such as 'The wolf is bitten'. But somewhere between age six and six and a half, children had acquired the knowledge that two deep structures were possible. They no longer always showed the named animal doing the biting, but neither did they interpret all the sentences in the adult manner. They would get some right and some wrong. Furthermore, when tested on two consecutive days, some of the sentences they got right one day, they would get wrong the next, and some they got wrong, they would now get right! It seems that although they knew that two different deep structures were possible, they had not yet mastered the second kind of learning — learning which words necessitated which interpretations. Finally, at about age nine or ten, children performed in the adult manner on all sentences.

Why children at about age six give up a rule of always interpreting these sentences as if the surface structure subject were the actor is a mystery. The change is probably related to other more general mental properties since it occurs so standardly at a particular mental age. Even children of subnormal intelligence change their rule systems as regards this structure at mental age six, in spite of the fact that chronologically they may be nine, ten, or eleven years of age.

The next part of the experiment was designed to examine the second kind of learning in which the structural properties of the particular words had to be acquired. It might be thought that children learn this structure through the acquisition of new *meanings*. It is difficult to know what could be meant by this. For example, what could be learned about the meaning of 'fun' that would allow the nine-year-old child to know that in 'The duck is fun to bite' it is the wolf who is doing the biting and having fun, while the five- or six-year-old believes that it means that the duck is having fun biting the wolf? The difference appears to be solely in the referent of 'fun', and that knowledge would appear to depend on how the word 'fun' is categorised.

Rather than a semantic process, it may be that a more purely grammatical learning is taking place. Take, for example, two words which 'point to' different deep structure interpretations when used in this structure. In 'The duck is *glad* to bite' the duck does the biting, but in 'The duck is *fun* to bite' it is the wolf who does the biting.

Another thing that can be noted about these two words is that they are differentially allowed or excluded by other sentence types. For example, one can say such sentences as 'I'm always *glad* to read to you', while 'I'm always *fun* to read to you' is ungrammatical. Similarly, sentences like 'Reading to you is *fun*' are acceptable, but sentences like 'Reading to you is *glad*' are not. Do children learn the structural properties of words like 'glad' and 'fun' by hearing them in related transformational sentence frames?

In a series of experiments, I presented children and adults with nonsense words in the differentiating frames. They then had to perform the action with the puppets when these same nonsense words were used in the test sentence: 'The wolf (or duck) is —— to bite'. The results were inconclusive as to whether this was the method by which such learning occurs. However, an interesting observation emerged from some of the answers. A fair number of those tested would use 'response strategies'. Such strategies were credited whenever an individual gave identical answers to all of six nonsense word tests. One strategy consisted of always showing the named animal as doing the biting, regardless of whether it was the wolf or the duck. The youngest children, of course, used this strategy, as they did even on sentences using real words. But whereas nearly half of the adults also used such a strategy, the older children almost never did. Instead, many of them used a curious strategy of always showing the non-named animal as doing the biting. One possibility is that they are using a strategy that is related to a linguistic universal which holds that if new linguistic information is made available concerning particular structures, one should treat these structures as if the basic expected grammatical ralationships have changed.

This is really an oversimplification based on some particular linguistic notions to do with what are called 'marked' and 'unmarked' forms, but what it essentially means in this case is that children hearing a new nonsense word in this frame will assume that a change in the basic grammatical relationships has occurred, and that the surface subject is no longer the actor as it would normally be. What is interesting about this strategy is that it is never used by adults. Can it be that children bring to bear on the language acquisition task certain methods of analysis which adults are either unable or at least unlikely to use?

Universals of language

If strategies like these are indeed used by children during a 'critical period' for language acquisition (see Lewin, Chapter 18) it would help to explain why children find learning language, even several languages at once, easier than adults struggling to learn a second language. It might also help us to understand why certain linguistic phenomena are found to exist nearly universally in the languages of the world. It might give us a clue as to the nature of the possibly innate language acquisition device that some linguists like Chomsky have postulated. And it might throw some light on the problems posed by children who do not acquire language in the normal manner. It may of course be that strategies like these are really a much more general cognitive phenomenon, rather than being specifically linguistic. But in that case it is difficult to see why adults fail to use them.

I have focused attention on one type of learning which may be specific to language. I am planning experiments to see if there are other specifically linguistic mechanisms which the child uses. Of course it is obvious that non-linguistic factors are also vitally important during the acquisition of language. General cognitive abilities, semantics (the referential and meaningful aspects of language) and pragmatics (how language is used as a communication system and to accomplish what purposes) all play an essential part in the process.

Cognitive abilities underlying language acquisition become clear when one studies children who have difficulty acquiring language. Some groups have been found to have a restricted short term memory capacity, thus severely affecting their ability to process utterances beyond a rather limited length. Other children may have impairments in the basic ability to attach meaning to sound. Still others may have difficulty in analysing the sounds they hear. And, as suggested above, it may be that some children suffer from an impairment in some type of 'language acquisition device' which prevents them from easily acquiring a grammatical system.

Jean Piaget has shown the importance of more complex thought processes underlying language. Many linguists and psycholinguists have also begun to emphasise the semantic and meaningful aspects in the acquisition of grammar. Jerome Bruner is undertaking a careful analysis of mother-child interaction which focuses on the pragmatics of a communication system (see Bruner, Chapter 6).

All of these levels—the cognitive, the semantic, the pragmatic, and the purely grammatical—must be explored and understood in order fully to understand how the normal child acquires language and to help with the various disabilities which occur in different children who do not acquire language. No particular theory is necessarily 'wrong' as one often infers from reading the disputes among these various theorists and their approaches to language. They are all partial theories.

We don't know how children acquire language, but at least we have reached the stage where we know we don't know. And that makes research in this area more exciting, more open, and in the long run more fruitful.

COGNITIVE DEVELOPMENT

Born with a high degree of native endowment, the human infant has the potential to acquire new knowledge, skills and competences from the very moment of birth. Within weeks of coming into the world a baby has built up an internal pattern of the most familiar feature in his environment: the mother's face. The baby can recognise the face and knows the voice associated with it, so much so that if the 'wrong' voice is presented with the familiar face he reacts against the false information.

Babies a few months old can work out tasks that require controlled head or sucking movements to produce a specific effect. Later, the infant learns skilled movements of the limbs, and finally comes to master abstract ideas.

Competent newborns

TOM BOWER

The human newborn is one of the most fascinating organisms
that a psychologist can study. It is only after birth that psychological processes can begin, that success and failure, reward
and punishment can begin to affect the development of the
child. Before that point function and practice—for many theorists the motor forces in development—have no opportunity
to modify the processes of growth that produce the neural
structures in the brain that must underpin any capacities that
are present at birth. The newborn infant is thus the natural
focus of the age-old and continuing controversy between nativists and empiricists: that is, the argument over whether human
knowledge is a natural endowment, like the structure of our
hand, with differences in intellectual competence as genetically
determined as differences in eye colour; or whether it is rather
the product of behaviour and experience in the world, with
differences in intellectual capacity a function of differences
in the quality of environmental exposure. An extreme proponent of the latter viewpoint would argue that the newborn,
with no exposure history behind him, should therefore show
no capacities at all, beyond the capacity to learn. Nativists
would have to predict something very different.

To the casual eye the empiricists would seem to have the
argument. The newborn seems extremely helpless, capable
of little save eating, sleeping and crying. But the casual eye
would be in error. The human newborn is an extremely competent organism, more competent than those of us brought
up in the British Empiricist tradition would ever have suspect-
ed. There are a number of precautions that one must take before
trying to study newborn humans. The methods that we use
to find out what newborns know must be adapted to characteristics of this fascinating organism. Obviously, no one would
sit and ask a newborn questions and expect to get many answers,

although as William Condon shows (Chapter 8), one can get fascinating information from such a procedure. However a newborn would not tell us in words how the world looked to him, for the obvious reason that newborns do not talk. If we want to find out what newborns know about the world, what they expect it to be like, we must rely on inferences from their behaviours.

We could not make many inferences about the newborns' knowledge of the world from observations of the spontaneous behaviour of babies in western culture. They have very few behaviours, and those that they have are not given much chance to appear in standard western baby-care conditions. For example, newborns have some quite precise head and eye movements and hand and arm movements in their repertoire. However, when the baby is laid on his back, a standard examination position, these behaviours virtually disappear. They disappear because the baby, in this position, must use his head and arms to hold himself in a stable position. If he picks up one arm to reach for something, he will roll in that direction. Even a head movement can result in a loss of postural equilibrium. The problem is compounded if the baby is wearing a large wad of nappies/diapers which tilt his weight up towards his head anyway. It follows that if one wants to use these head and eye and arm and hand behaviours to index the baby's knowledge of the world, one must place the baby in a position that allows him to move head and arms freely. In experiments in my lab we use makeshift arrangements of pillows to accomplish this, although more sophisticated baby chairs are available.

A second problem with newborns is not so easily solved. That is the problem of wakefulness. Newborns are awake for very brief periods, about six minutes at a time. At other times they may look awake, with eyes open and so on, and yet be functionally asleep. Without sophisticated apparatus to measure brain-waves and other psycho-physiological variables, it is hard to be sure that one is dealing with a fully awake baby. Lastly if the baby is not fully awake there seems to be no way of waking him up. Prechtl has presented evidence that the sleeping-waking cycles of newborns are under internal control and are relatively impervious to external events. Certainly, in my laboratory we have found that loud noises, flicks on the sole of the foot, and other techniques all fail to wake a baby who has gone off to sleep. In working with newborns, more than at any later stage of human development, the investigator must await the convenience of his subject.

The traditional starting point for an analysis of knowledge is the input that comes in through the senses (sight, sound, smell and touch, for example). That input does not seem capable of providing the information that adults are able to get out of it. Psychologists have assumed that the deficiencies in the sensory input were made up by learning and experience. But recent experiments with newborns must cast some doubt on this point of view.

Consider, for instance, the ability to localise an odour. Adults can localise odours, to right or left, with a fair degree of accuracy. This is a problem for psychology. Because there is no right or left in the nose, the right-left dimension of experience must be elaborated from other information. There are of course two sources of relevant information: the different intensities of odour at the two nostrils (an odour source on the right will stimulate the right nostril with greater intensity than it will the left); and the different times of arrival of the odour-producing molecules at the nostrils, a source on the right reaching the right nostril fractionally before it reaches the left. These time/intensity differences are used by the perceptual system to specify position to right and left. The structure that does this is present in newborns, who will turn smoothly away from 'unpleasant' odour sources, indicating that they are capable of olfactory localisation, as well as sharing adults' opinions of the pleasantness of some odours.

The auditory system poses similar problems. Adults can locate sounds to right and left with great precision, although there is no right and left within the auditory system. Perception of position of a sound source is elaborated from differences in the time of arrival and in intensity between the two ears, as well as patterns of reflection set up in the outer ear.

Michael Wertheimer demonstrated that within seconds of birth infants can use this information, turning their eyes correctly towards a sound source. This shows not only auditory localisation, but also auditory-visual coordination, an expectation that there will be something to be seen at a sound source.

My colleague Eric Aronson has confirmed the same basic point in more complicated experiments performed in Edinburgh. While an infant is in special apparatus, he can see his mother through the soundproof glass screen, but can only hear her via the two speakers of a stereo system. The balance on the stereo can be adjusted to make the sound appear to come from straight ahead or any other position. If the mother speaks to her baby with the balance adjusted so that the heard voice appears to come from her seen mouth, the baby is quite happy. But if the heard voice and seen mouth do not coincide, very young infants manifest surprise and upset, indicating auditory localisation, auditory-visual coordination, and, more surprisingly, an expectation that voices will come from mouths. This is an example of competence that seems to be lost with age. In lecture theatres or cinemas, for example, where heard voice and seen mouth are often in very different places, adults do not seem to be aware of the discrepancy.

The study of auditory localisation is also important in that it allows us to begin to define the limits of innate structuring and to indicate just what perceptual capacities do require information from the environment. I said earlier that perception of position of a sound source is generated from differences in time of arrival and intensity between the two ears. Consider how time of arrival differences function in auditory localisation. A sound source which is straight ahead of an observer emits sound waves which reach both ears simultaneously. A sound source which is to the right emits sound waves which reach the right ear before the left ear. A sound source on the left emits sound waves which reach the left ear before the right ear.

The further away a sound source is from the midline (to the left or right), the greater is the difference between time of arrival at the leading ear and time of arrival at the following ear. Human adults use these time of arrival differences to compute the precise position of a sound source.

Time of arrival differences do not depend simply on the position of the sound source—they also depend on the distance between the two ears. The further apart ears are, the greater will be the time of arrival difference produced by a given deviation from the midline plane. Newborn babies' ears are obviously much closer together than are the ears of human adults. As the baby grows, the ears become further apart as the head gets bigger. This raises the question of whether the newborn 'knows' how far apart his ears are. In auditory localisation the newborn shares some information with the adult. That information is that (1) zero time of arrival differences signify that a sound source is in the midline plane (straight ahead or straight behind); (2) when the right ear is stimulated before the left, the sound source is on the right and vice-versa. These two items of information are invariant during growth. The information about the precise value to be attached to any given time of arrival difference, by contrast, changes during growth.

There are thus two types of information involved in auditory localisation, one being dependent on growth, the other being independent. It seems obvious that the baby's genetic blueprint could incorporate the growth-independent information without too much trouble. It seems less likely that the growth-dependent information could be so incorporated, especially since the growth of the head depends on the quality of nutrition available to the growing child (see Chapter 17).

Experimentation has shown this armchair speculation to be correct. We have done a variety of experiments on the precision of auditory localisation of sound sources in various positions. In one set of experiments we put babies in a light-tight dark room and then introduced noise-making objects at various positions around the baby. We compared his performance in this situation with his performance in a situation where the baby could see the object continuously, or else where he was shown the object briefly before the lights were switched out. When the noise-making object was straight ahead babies could localise it as or more accurately than they could localise a seen object. If the object was on the right they localised it to the right— if it was on the left they localised it to the left. However, the precision of their localisation to the right or left in the dark was very poor indeed, much poorer than it was with either continuous or momentary visual information about the location of the object.

We conclude from these results that if the information required for a perceptual task is growth-independent, it will be inbuilt (in the genes); if the information is growth-dependent, however, it will have to be acquired through experience in the environment, it has to be learnt. In our experiments, babies did not seem to acquire this growth-dependent information until they were about seven months old. Not until that age did the precision of their reaching for a sound source off the midline attain the precision of their reaching for a sound source on the midline, or the precision of their reaching for a seen target in any location.

The hypothesis that growth-invariant information is built-in and that growth-dependent information must be acquired, has proved useful in analysing visual development and the coordination of hand and eye. The size of the eye changes as the baby grows, as does the distance between the eyes. Distance between the eyes is critical for three-dimensional vision. Our experiments indicate again that it is necessary for the baby to have some experience in the world before he can use this growth-dependent information precisely. Similar problems crop up in reaching itself, where the length of arm changes drastically during growth. Very young babies do not seem to know precisely how long their arms are, reaching for objects that are out of reach and reaching past objects that are within reach.

Vision itself has attracted rather more attention than the other senses, reflecting its greater importance in normal function. Although the eye is a more elaborate structure than the nose or ear, with a built-in structure to register right-left position, for example, there are many dimensions of visual experience that do not seem to be given directly in the visual input. For example, visual experience is clearly three-dimensional, and the third dimension, distance, is missing from the input to the eye (Figure 1). Beginning with Bishop Berkeley

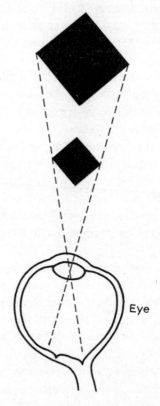

Figure 1   The retina, a two-dimensional surface, obviously cannot register three-dimensional variables, such as distance, size or shape.

in the eighteenth century, empiricists have assumed that distance could only be gauged after man had learned to interpret clues for distance. It now seems that the interpretation of these signs, if this is what occurs, need not be learned.

With colleagues in America I discovered that infants can demonstrate adjustments to the distance of objects during the newborn period. For example, if one moves an object towards the face of a baby he will execute a well-coordinated defensive movement, pulling back his head and bringing his hands and arms between himself and the object. The response occurs whether or not the object used is a real object, like the one shown in the figure, or a purely visual simulation projected on a screen. The latter result indicates that the response is only elicited if the approaching objects come within a certain distance, which seems to be about thirty centimetres. Approach closer than this distance elicits defensive movements, even if the approaching object is small. Approach which stops further away than thirty centimetres will not elicit defensive movements, even if the approaching object is large. This indicates that the infants are not responding simply to the size of the retinal image produced by the approaching object.

The fact that infants seem to defend themselves against the approach of seen objects seems indicative, at least, of some expectation that seen objects are tangible. I have obtained more convincing evidence of such an expectation by presenting the infant with virtual objects, objects which are visible yet intangible. Two devices that will produce such objects are shown in Figure 2. One depends on the presence of a functioning binocular vision system in the infant (Figure 2a). Two oppositely polarised beams of light cast a double shadow of an object on a rear projection screen. An infant views the double shadows through polarising goggles that make a different shadow visible to each eye. The innate processes of stereopsis fuse the two images to make the infant think he is seeing a solid object in front of the screen. The other depends on nothing more than simple optics (Figure 2b).

Newborn infants will reach out to touch seen objects. The behaviour is very crude but does result in a high proportion of contacts if a real object is presented. What happens if a virtual object is presented? When the infant's hand reaches the seen location of the object there is no tactual input, since the object

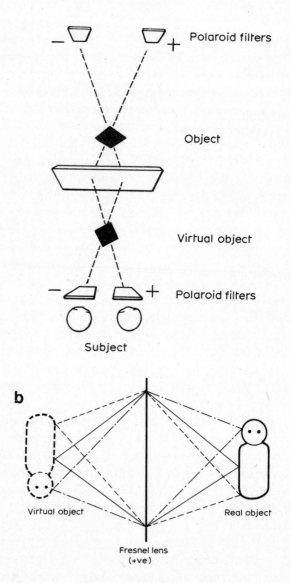

Figure 2 (a) and (b) Two devices for producing a virtual object (a) using a shadow caster (b) using a positive fresnel lens.

is intangible. If the infant expects seen objects to be tangible, this event should surprise him, as indeed it does. Infants presented with such objects react with extreme surprise and upset, indicating some degree of visual-tactual coordination.

In a recent experiment in my laboratory Jane Dunkeld has shown a similar discrimination using the defensive response to an approaching object that was described above. If babies are presented with an approaching object they defend themselves. If they are presented with an approaching aperture, which would pass them by harmlessly, they do not defend themselves. They thus discriminate between things and the spaces between things, and can tell what type of information specifies the two types of display. The information they are picking up is quite subtle. It seems that approaching objects cover up background texture while approaching apertures reveal it, a delicate discrimination that newborns can make.

None of the capacities described above would be at all obvious to a casual eye. They cannot be elicited from infants save in conditions which are somewhat special in our culture. The infant must be propped up and his head and arms must be free to move. This condition is not met if the baby is lying flat on his back, the most common position for baby observation in this culture. A newborn on his back uses head and arms to support himself in a stable position. Thus neither is free to engage in any of the indicator behaviours described above.

The experiments I have described so far indicate that newborn infants have a functioning perceptual system, with a striking degree of coordination between the senses. The last experiments on this line that I wish to mention provide the most striking instance of such coordinations: a coordination between vision and the baby's own body image. If a human adult seats himself or herself in front of a newborn infant (three weeks old) and engages in any of a wide variety of face or finger movements, the infant will imitate the adult's movements. If the adult sticks his tongue out, the baby will retaliate. If the adult opens and closes his mouth repetively, the baby will mimic the movements. Babies as young as this have no experience of mirrors, and yet they know they have a mouth and a tongue and can match the seen mouth and tongue of an adult to their own unseen mouth and tongue, a most striking demonstration of intersensory matching. The infant perceives a match, a similarity, between himself and adults, a capacity of immense significant for all development, and particularly social development.

So far I have spoken of capacities that seem to be innate. I have not mentioned the one capacity that empiricists would maintain must be innate—the capacity to learn. The learning abilities of the newborn infant have been a major focus of research. Since new behaviours do appear at a great rate throughout infancy, it is important, theoretically, to establish that learning can occur, and could therefore account for the emergent behaviours. Eight years ago it seemed that research had failed to demonstrate that the infant of less than six months can learn anything at all. This pessimistic conclusion has been totally overthrown since then to the extent that it has even been suggested that the newborn infant can learn better at that point in his development than he ever will again.

Psychologists assess learning with very simple paradigms involving rewards for specific activities. Increase in the rate of the rewarded activity is taken as a measure of learning. The problem is to make sure that the reward is really rewarding. If one can do this with infants they will readily demonstrate learning of a high order. Unfortunately, older infants are readily bored with most rewards. A few studies have used food, supplementary to normal diet, to elicit performance. Many more experimenters have used presentation of visual events to motivate the infant. The motivational problem seems simpler with very young babies. In the first few days of life one can demonstrate learning of a very high order. Neonate infants can learn not one but a *pair* of response-reward contingencies, requiring two different responses signalled by two different stimuli. For instance, Lew Lipsett, of Brown University, and I discovered separately that a three-day-old infant can learn to turn his head to the left to obtain reward when a bell sounds, and to the right when a buzzer sounds. He can learn the bell-left, buzzer-right discrimination in a few minutes. Having learned it he can learn to reverse the discrimination if the experimenter reverses the contingencies, to go bell-right, buzzer-left, again very rapidly. The learning displayed here is possibly of a higher order than is ever displayed by an infra-human.

Born with a high native endowment, the human infant has the potential to acquire new knowledge, skills and competences from the very moment of birth. The newborn thus forces us to a compromise between nativism and empiricism, possessing as he does enough capacity to make rapid learning possible.

The newborn may have done more than merely make us compromise, however, he may have forced us to reconsider the whole concept of development. A foundation that under-pins the bulk of developmental psychology is the assumption that development is a continuous, step-by-step process, with older organisms knowing all that younger organisms know, plus some surplus. Appreciation of what happens to many of the capacities described above should make us reconsider this basic assumption. Many of the capacities of the newborn fade away in the course of development, some of them never to return. Neonate walking, a phenomenon I have not described, is a case in point. If newborns are held properly, they march along a solid surface in a most impressive manner. This capacity disappears at about the age of eight weeks. The reaching of newborns disappears at about the age of four weeks. Their ability, or perhaps willingness, to imitate goes at about the same time. I have already mentioned the loss of auditory-visual coordination in Aronson type situations. That capacity goes in the first few months of life and does not come back, seemingly, since, as I said, most adults simply do not notice auditory-visual discrepancy.

Similar problems occur with auditory localisation. I mentioned that young babies will reach for a noise-making object in darkness, albeit somewhat inaccurately. In the course of development this coordination disappears. Babies over six months are very unlikely to reach for a noise-making object in darkness. In some cases the coordination does not reappear at all, so that the child becomes motorically paralysed in total darkness. The simplest explanation of such losses of capacity would be that the capacities are simply not used and so atrophy from lack of use, as neural connections will.

That cannot be the whole explanation since practice cannot stop the decline in walking or reaching. It can slow it but it cannot arrest it completely. The decline in hand-ear coordination cannot be stopped by practice either. Giving a baby a great deal of experience in darkness with noise-making objects will not arrest the drop in hand-ear coordination. Indeed I have heard of one study of a blind baby who nonetheless lost the capacity right on schedule, despite a great deal of opportunity to use the coordination, and despite the fact that the baby was then left with no other sensory system to guide him in the world.

The loss of capacities under such conditions argues against simple lack of practice as an explanation. It seems rather as if some genetically determined developmental process is switching off the coordinations, despite environmental attempts to keep them switched on. The function of such a process is quite obscure. Its existence would seem to call into question the whole rationale for studies of very young infants. What is the point of studying them if their abilities are going to be switched off in the course of development? I have no ready answers to that question. However, there is some very exciting evidence that indicates that what happens to these capacities while they are present may specify the rate and course of later development.

Researchers have discovered that infants whose neonate walking is practised will walk sooner than infants who have not been so practised. Infants whose reaching ability has been utilised in the neonate period produce true reaching earlier than infants who have not had such practice. Infants who have used hand-ear coordination extensively prior to its disappearance are more likely to recover the capacity than infants who have not had such practice, indicating that not only rate but also direction of development may be determined by the environment that these early capacities have. It is this possibility that makes the study of newborn capacities and their subsequent history in the world such an exciting area at the moment. Newborns are very similar to each other. Older children and adults are very different. It is possible that the effect of the environment on newborn capacities has a disproportionate influence on the development of such differences.

Mother's face and the newborn
GENEVIEVE CARPENTER

How aware is a newborn baby? In the first few days of life, babies have a surprising degree of sophistication in response to the environment. The normal full-term neonate is capable of processing information received through all sensory systems. In the laboratory infants show discrimination, habituation, response to novelty and conditioning. This picture of the newborn baby has developed over the past dozen years from the research of many investigators.

For a very long time doctors believed that until the age of about six weeks babies cannot see in any real sense. But psychologists now know that within the very first days of life infants can see well enough to respond differently to stimuli with differing physical characteristics. For example, they look at black and white patterns, such as a set of stripes as narrow as an eighth of an inch, for longer than an unpatterned gray patch of equal brightness; or at a black-on-white line drawing of a face for longer than three black dots on white. When they see the same pattern over and over again, they actively turn away and spend less and less time looking as trials progress. When a novel pattern is then presented, many infants become interested once again.

A baby's reaction to sound can be detected in changes of muscle activity, heart-rate, and breathing, for example. Newborns are sensitive to various different sounds. For instance, they respond to patterned (square wave) tones and to the human voice more readily than to pure (sine wave) tones. For patterned and pure tones the most effective ones have fundamental frequencies within the range of the human voice. When a baby's response has diminished with repeated presentations of a given tone, a tone of a different frequency, or the same tone at an increased amplitude, produces a renewed response.

Visual attention in newborns

Since Robert Fantz, Western Reserve University, first demonstrated in the early 1960s that babies could distinguish between visually presented patterns in the first few days of life, a flood of research activity has followed, teasing out the capabilities and limitations of the human newborn's visual system, and the principles operating to determine their selective attention. Fantz and his colleagues, soon followed by many other investigators, only some of whose work I mention here, uses an ingeniously humble tool: he simply measures the amount of time infants spend looking at patterns or objects of different physical characteristics under controlled conditions. Sometimes he presents stimuli singly and sometimes in pairs, the latter yielding visual 'preferences'. Typically the stimuli are shown at seven to ten inches from a baby's eyes, which, on the basis of present evidence, gives the sharpest image in the early days of life.

William Kessen, at Yale University, and his colleagues have used infrared corneal photography to measure where neonates' fixations are concentrated on simple black and white, two-dimensional geometric stimuli such as triangles. Their results suggest that angles and edges, for example, are basic elements to which newborns respond and from which an infant constructs shapes and patterns. Meanwhile, Bernard Karmel, now at the University of Connecticut, who experiments with black and white checkerboards and related stimuli, finds that infants' attention to patterns can be precisely stated as a mathematical function of black-white boundaries in a pattern (it is a curvilinear function of the square root of the total length of all the boundaries).

Tom Bower and his colleagues, some in America and others in Edinburgh, have approached the question of visual perception from a different tack (see Chapter 11). They are examining the extent to which the young infant sees the world much as an adult does. Bower finds that the young infant 'perceives objects of some size in space at some distance.' For example,

different stimuli projecting the same retinal image size have
been produced either by a solid object and its two-dimensional
representation (a photograph) or by two three-dimensional
objects varied in size and distance from the baby's eyes. In the
second week of life, babies' reaching and grasping responses
were appropriate to the actual size and distance of objects, not
retinal image size. And the infants did not reach for the photograph. This evidence suggests that the newborn, perhaps from
birth, experiences a three-dimensional world.

The human face

Another approach has been to examine perceptual capacities
with reference to aspects of the infant's everyday life. It seemed
that babies' most sophisticated performance might be found
in relation to things they experience repeatedly. In the visual
sphere, from birth, the 'object' occurring most frequently at
focal distance is the human face. Psychologists knew little
about the newborn baby's capacity for processing information
from highly complex three-dimensional coloured objects such
as faces. However, granted a system ready to respond to many
aspects of the environment, the repetitive nature of a newborn's care, and the importance to the infant of its mother, it
seemed reasonable to study response to the mother's face under
controlled conditions during the very early weeks of life. With
colleagues at Boston University Medical School, I therefore
asked the simple question: Can newborns respond to any
differences between three-dimensional facial forms?

In the laboratory we observed normal, full-term Negro
female newborns selected for being visually alert; the tests
were carried out once a week from age one week through to
eight weeks. (We chose female infants because male and
female infants, on average, respond to some perceptual tasks
differently and have different rates of development, with
females often ahead.) When calm and alert, a baby was made
comfortable in an infant seat with soft pillows located in a well-
lighted, unpatterned, semi-enclosure at ten to twelve inches
from a door which could open to display a face (Figure 1).

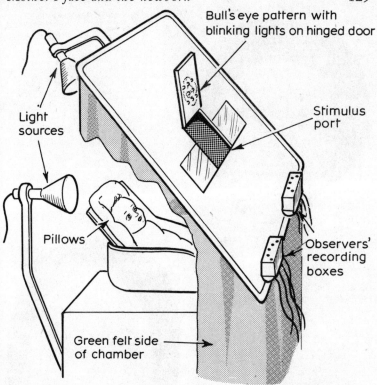

Figure 1   Apparatus for presenting stimuli to infants.

Under appropriately ordered conditions each baby saw, for a
fixed time, the mother's face, a shop model's face and an
abstract 'facial' form—a kitchen collander bent to an oval shape
and painted flesh colour, with three coloured knobs attached
to create 'features' (Figure 2). Experimenters, observing from
the darkened outer laboratory and therefore unseen by the
infant, could record whether the baby was looking directly at
a face, looking off-target, turning right away, or closing its
eyes. The answer to the question posed (can infants discriminate between three-dimensional facial forms) was 'yes': by
two weeks of age infants looked reliably longer when either
artificial 'face' was displayed than when the mother was
shown.

Figure 2 The three 'faces' shown to infants.

We were surprised to find *least* attention to the frequently experienced mother's face. However, the nature of the behaviour which produced the results was not evident in the attention data alone. Each time a face was presented, the infant typically looked toward and away from it in active involvement. This was in direct contrast to the sustained attention to dimly blinking lights displayed on the door which closed in the interval between faces. The lesser attention to the mother was neither passive uninterest nor active search for other information. Infants would tense as they averted their gaze, appearing to keep the target in peripheral view. From this position they would frequently take furtive glances. Sometimes they would turn ninety degrees and cry. Thus, attention did not tell the whole story. Even the non-looking behaviour seemed purposeful. Although the infants appeared to be avoiding contact with the mother, it was just possible that the darker faces of Negro mothers provided less distinct contrasts and contours and were simply more difficult to fixate.

This question of stimulus brightness and contrasts was answered in my next study, which was concerned primarily with the role of stimulus movement in very early attention. Three faces were again presented (shown both stationary and moving horizontally) but this time the mother's faces were Caucasian and, on average, of equivalent brightness to the shop model's face. I also added a Negroid model (Figure 2). I selected Caucasian infants on the criteria used in the previous study and observed under similar conditions.

This new sample of infants also looked least at the mother. Moreover, at each age, the average number of seconds spent looking at mother when stationary was virtually the same for the two samples. When the faces moved they all attracted more attention. But even when faces moved, mother was looked at least. Both Caucasian and Negroid models received more attention than mother, but there was not a reliable difference in response to the two models. (Absence of differential response to the two models does not here imply inability to discriminate between them.) Thus I could eliminate stimulus brightness as the basis of differential response. And the strange phenomenon of more turning from direct regard of the live face of the infant's mother was repeatable. On whatever basis infants were discriminating, it was something that faces of widely differing physical characteristics (the infants' mothers) had in common with each other and not with the models. The common element may be familiarity from repeated experience.

Jerome Kagan, now at Harvard, and colleagues have reported that older infants than those considered here, deploy their attention in accordance with a 'discrepancy principle'. They postulate that an infant's repeated experience of a particular event results in an internally stored representation ('schema') of that event. According to the discrepancy hypothesis, children at any stage of development will give their attention longer to stimuli which are moderately divergent from a newly developing schema than to those that are very discrepant or very familar.

Detecting incongruity

A number of psychologists, including Daniel Berlyne and J. McV. Hunt, have evolved theory which relates animal and human behaviour to motivation. On this theory, arousal and attention increase as incongruity increases up to an optimum point. Beyond that, any further increase causes a reduction in attention or withdrawal. This appears to be a mechanism for reducing arousal and discrepancy to a comfortable level. The question arose: did the babies in my experiments behave as they did for the reasons outlined by this theory?

A very high percentage of a newborn baby's entire experience of the world includes the mother. Normally, mother's face moves animatedly, and is accompanied by talking, touching and moving. When her face appears in a small opening surrounded by unpatterned green felt and does nothing, or at best moves rhythmically, might it not be familiar in itself, and yet highly discrepant with reference to the infant's everyday experience of it? One is reminded of Donald Hebb's chimpanzees who shrank from a very realistic modelled head of a chimp with no body and from an anaesthetised chimp lacking responsiveness. Similarly, infants' turning away might be understood as visual withdrawal from a situation of high incongruity. This line of reasoning suggests that the infants looked at mother least because she was a familiar object in an unfamiliar context; again, the response may be a visual withdrawal from an incongruous situation.

If turning away is indeed visual withdrawal from the incongruous, one would expect less and less looking away the more closely the experimental conditions conform to the usual. For example, one would expect less turning away and therefore more attention if the mother talked to the baby. On the other hand, if the mother's face were accompanied by a voice not her own, or if her voice accompanied some other face, this would be incongruous and produce marked turning away. This would happen only if the particular face and voice of the mother were both being learned.

As a first step toward testing the possibility of such very early learning (recognition of face and voice) I recently carried out an experiment with a group of normal, full-term, visually active female infants born in St Mary's Hospital (Paddington), London. I observed them once a week in the Behaviour Development Research Unit, from age two weeks through to seven weeks. Under the same experimental circumstances described earlier, I measured infants' responses to a number of situations: the mother's face alone, as in previous studies; mother's face plus mother's voice; mother's face with a stranger's voice; and parallel conditions for stranger's face. (Faces were live, voices were tape recorded. The 'speaker' mimed the words.)

The overriding differentiation made by the infants was between mother's face and a stranger's face; this differentiation occurred as early as two weeks of age. (No observations were made prior to this age.) Mother's face, in this experiment, received more attention than stranger's face regardless of voice conditions. Indeed, each face was looked at longer if accompanied by a voice, but mother's face without voice was more attention-attracting than stranger's face with either voice. These same differentiations were found in the very first ocular fixation of each thirty-second facial presentation. Most turning right away from direct regard (beyond forty-five degrees from midline) occurred when faces and voices were 'mismatched'.

Clearly the infants in this selected group were capable of detecting difference between two live female faces during the earliest weeks of life. Whatever cues the infants were using—salient features or the whole configuration—they were sufficient to allow discrimination in the first fixation. More turning right away from a face with mismatching voice indicates that voices were also discriminated and suggests that associations between the familiar face and voice had been learned. Both visual and auditory information appear to be compared with an internal model established very early through experience. The findings are broadly compatible with the hypothesis that the more 'normal' the conditions, the more attention infants will pay.

Comparing the three studies, attention to mother's stationary face was very much the same. Attention to stranger's stationary face also showed the same trend in preliminary work with an earlier sample who on average looked less at a stranger (one of two other ladies used as experimental stranger) than at mother. Yet the two types of non-mother faces received different response: the artificial faces were looked at more than mother, and the female stranger less than mother. This suggests that sensory input may undergo a process of multiple categorisation—for example, familiar/strange, animate/inanimate, and even odour/no-odour—which mediates attention.

Sophisticated information processing

Infants at this very early age are generally assumed to be able to respond only to immediate sensory events. On the basis of my findings it now seems that they are also able to screen sensory input with reference to information stored from everyday experience. Further, it appears that more than one category may be used in classifying information. It may also be that infants do not have to build their picture of the world from scratch, by piecing together angles and contours, for example, but see configurations which become elaborated and refined in the course of development. More sophisticated information-processing capabilities appear to be operating in the newborn's interaction with its environment than we had thought possible.

These results raise further questions about the beginning of social attachment. The development of a first emotional bond depends upon the infant's familiarisation with a particular person—usually the mother. Although it is commonly accepted that an infant shows signs of recognising its mother within the first six months of life, clear-cut discrimination of an unfamiliar person has been found repeatedly by six to eight months of age. At this time, infants respond negatively to strangers, for example, by looking away, turning away, or whimpering. These withdrawal behaviours are construed as 'stranger anxiety'. According to the theoretical formulations mentioned earlier, withdrawal arises when there is incongruity between immediate sensory input and some schema stored within the brain. Only when such a central representation has been established, through repeated exposure, can incongruity be perceived. Therefore, withdrawal from strangers, consistently found in the second half of the first year, has sometimes been taken to indicate the earliest point at which the infant has a permanent representation of mother which allows her to be not only recognised as familiar, but also recalled in her absence as a standard against which other persons are compared and found strange.

Newborn babies' apparent withdrawal reactions described in the St Mary's study are very similar to those interpreted as 'stranger anxiety' in older infants. Yet, in this experiment, the mother and stranger occurred, not simultaneously for comparison, but separately in time. Thus, newborns' greater turning away from the stranger could be an early manifestation of this same process of matching sensory input against a stored representation commonly thought not to occur until some months later in development. Perhaps by distorting the newborn's 'normal' experience through controlled laboratory conditions, basic cognitive processes underlying social bonding have been revealed much earlier in development than has been possible by observations in the home or clinic. The alternating acceptance and fear of strangers found as the weeks and months pass may indicate cycles of generalisation and discrimination as mental development proceeds.

In conclusion, from the earliest days the newborn infant plays an active role in selecting the stimulation to which he will attend. This selection depends upon inbuilt functional characteristics of the organism, external stimulus properties, and at some point in development, upon memories and associations from experience. My recent work on infants' responses to faces and voices suggests that experience already plays a role within the first weeks of life.

The growth of skill

KEVIN CONNOLLY

It can be argued that the major task of childhood is to develop ways of exerting control over the environment. The ability to direct and influence events is very important to each of us in many ways. From birth throughout childhood, and indeed throughout our whole life, we acquire various means of accomplishing this. We achieve control and the power to influence circumstances and events by acquiring skills—social skills, intellectual skills and motor skills. Here, I shall discuss motor skills, though these have many attributes in common with intellectual skills and with problem solving.

When we describe a person as skilled we usually mean that he has mastered some task with a notable degree of efficiency and can perform it with economy. But note, that to say a person is skilled is not to make any absolute judgment. Driving a car, operating a lathe, writing, or playing tennis are all skilled activities and different people exhibit varying degrees of skill at different times and at different ages. In the course of everyday life we meet so many examples of skilled behaviour that it is perhaps not surprising that for the most part we ignore the commonplace and direct our attention to examples of outstanding performance. For the psychologist the concept of skill covers not only the abilities of the test cricketer, the concert pianist, the aircraft pilot and the sculptor, but also such common everyday behaviour as walking, grasping and turning a door knob, or signing one's name. The elements and essential ingredients found in the behaviour of world class performers are found also in the normal baby and toddler.

Typically, the motor behaviour of young infants appears staccato and halting when compared with the smoothly orchestrated performance of older children or of adults. The stumbling of the one-year-old as he attempts to walk is a suitable example. He staggers almost like the drunken man from one support to another, all his attention being absorbed in remaining upright for just a few moments. And yet within a short time the same youngster is able to run, chasing a ball, whilst calling out to another child. How does all of this come about? From studies of early and middle childhood we know that certain typical changes in performance occur. Children are able to perform movements more rapidly and with increasing accuracy. The trade-off between speed and accuracy also changes. Requiring that a child respond accurately, yet quickly, on a given task does not impose the same stress on the ten-year-old that it does on the five-year-old. Moreover children become able to take on tasks of increasing complexity which in some respects demand higher levels of skill. How this is achieved is the central problem of understanding the growth of skills.

The nature of skill

Like a number of familiar and important aspects of behaviour, skill is difficult to define in any fully adequate fashion. However, it is possible to identify certain attributes of skill and from these see more clearly what it is that we are dealing with. The meaning of the term skill as given by the dictionary points to a fundamental feature: to understand, to comprehend, to have knowledge of, to know how to do something. Skilled behaviour very obviously is directed towards the attainment of some goal in the environment; it may be picking up an object or driving a motor car. But whatever the example chosen we are concerned with cognitive activity, with a goal or series of goals towards which the behaviour is directed.

Skilled motor behaviour is concerned with the patterning of movements in time and in space, movements which make up a programme of action specifying an objective to be attained. The means-end relationship is a central feature of skilled performance and it is the ability to make adaptations in the means of attaining desired ends that characterises the skilled person. Flexibility in adjusting the means of achieving a given end to the changing characteristics and demands of the situation is one of the hallmarks of skill. Thus once a child has mastered walking he can do it on a pavement, in loose sand, snow, a ploughed field, up hill, down hill or on a flight of stairs. Although in each case the activity is walking, the environmental conditions and constraints vary greatly.

Another aspect of the flexibility of skilled behaviour is its creative attributes. The same goal may be achieved by employing a number of quite different combinations of movements. As I sit at my table writing this chapter I am carrying out several tasks with my hands. Holding a pen and making certain movements to produce symbols on the paper, packing and lighting a pipe, picking up a coffee cup, striking a match etcetera. For all of these activities I use my hands, and although all of them have features in common they are all distinctly different. It is necessary too to avoid confusing skill with movement. I can write the initial letter of my name with a pen held in my right hand but also if pressed I could do it with a pencil held between my teeth. In both cases the end product is essentially the same but the means of its achievement differ, as do the movements and muscles involved.

The structure of skill

In developing skills the child is involved in constructing programmes of action directed at particular ends; such activity, therefore, is purposeful and implies an *intention* on the part of the child. Now if we are to think of skills as action programmes, a basic question is concerned with the units which make up the programme. The whole sequence of sub-units, or sub-routines as they have been termed, is what we generally think of as the skill, walking, playing the piano or using cutlery. Analysing the skill into its component units, examining the manner in which the units are linked together and the way the rules governing the linkage are deployed offers us a way of studying the growth and structure of skill.

Let us consider an example which most young children will tackle. Imagine a three-year-old given a boiled egg for breakfast. The egg sits in its cup on the table, the top having been removed, and the child is given a suitable spoon. Before he can solve the problem the child must have an idea of what he is aiming at; in other words intention on his part is implied. Furthermore he must know something about the uses and properties of a spoon. Given these, let us examine what the task entails. The child must pick up the spoon and hold it both appropriately (a suitable position on the handle) and securely. Then he has to take it to the egg, which is quite a small target, and insert it. Once the spoon is in the egg its orientation has to be varied, and controlled force must be applied. Not too much force or the egg breaks apart, but enough to cut into the yolk and the harder white of the egg. There are in fact quite fine tolerance limits within which the child must operate. Having got egg onto the spoon the child now has to carry it back to his mouth, a target which he cannot see but which is already very familiar to him. The two components of the task which involve movement to targets, the egg and the mouth, are different since the constraints which apply to each of them differ. In carrying the egg to the mouth the spoon has to be held in a particular orientation or the egg is lost. Altogether this is a difficult and complex task as becomes clear from watching a young child battling with the problem.

The ultimate smooth performance shown by a child skilled on a task such as that described above depends upon his mastering a variety of sub-units or components which he then combines in various ways. Once a general plan emerges and the task is attempted, albeit very coarsely, then performance can be shaped and refined by practice. An approximately successful outcome is in itself rewarding and will lead to the refinement and adjustment of the sub-units and of the programme in which they are embedded. A further and crucially important consequence of practice is that the sub-routines themselves become increasingly reliable and predictable. As they are freed from a dependence on a particular context they assume a modular quality and can confidently be employed in different action programmes. For example, the adult grip on a pencil (see Figure 1), in which it is held between the thumb and first finger with the second finger serving as a stabilising support, once mastered can be used on other tools which require fine manipulation; a paint brush, a probe or a small

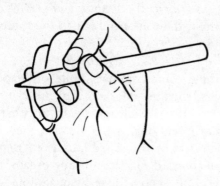

Figure 1   An adult grip on a pencil. Note how the finger and thumb are opposed to give free control.

screwdriver. There are other important consequences also because the adult grip pattern permits movements which other grips such as the palmar grip (see Figure 2) do not allow.

Figure 2   A palmar grip on a pencil.

Holding a pencil in an adult grip allows the small finger movements which I need in order to write cursive script. In the case of the palmar grip it is not possible to move the pencil relative to the hand, it can be moved only by moving the whole hand and arm relative to the body. In writing, both intrinsic movements, as I form the letters, and extrinsic movements, as I move across the page from left to right, are employed.

A model of skilled behaviour

Having in mind some common, quite ordinary examples of skilled activity, such as that described, we can now say more about the attributes of skill and begin to construct a model. The notion of intentionality implies that there is some form of plan which is to be translated into a programme of action. The plan is expressed via the effector organs in movements and postures, the success and adequacy of which must be evaluated in relation to the plan. This brings in the notion of feedback. Feedback can be classified into different types. There is the feedback from the receptors in muscles and tendons arising whilst a movement is in progress and there is also the feedback we obtain via other sense organs; for example, seeing what is happening as we carry out an action. As I write I have both kinds of feedback.

Another type of feedback, known to be important in learning, is called by psychologists 'knowledge of results'; this is terminal information telling us about the consequences of action. Seeing just where a dart lands when it is thrown at a dart board gives knowledge of results. Feedback is used to compare realised action with the intended plan: if there is a mismatch between the two, correction signals are used to modify the output at the effectors which in turn is monitored and evaluated. Several models of control systems embodying the feedback principle have been described and a number of them have been used to describe the regulation of motor behaviour. The basic logic is shown in Figure 3. The plan is used to generate instructions to effector organs, the muscular system, which gives rise to motor behaviour. The effects of the organism's behaviour upon the environment are picked up by receptor mechanisms (perceptual inputs through various sense modalities) and this external information along with information about the state of the effector mechanisms is sent to a comparator. The function of the comparator is to evaluate the realised against the intended action and if a mismatch occurs to signal the effectors with a correction.

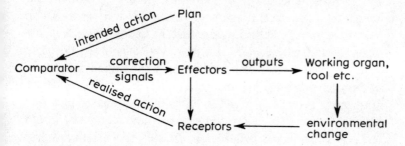

Figure 3 The basic logical components of a system with feedback control. The feedback via receptor mechanisms is compared with intended action from the plan. Any discrepancy between intended and realised actions detected by the comparator causes a correction signal to be sent to the effectors.

As a child grows the improvements in his motor skills reflect changes of various kinds. By analogy with a computer we can think of these as hardware and software factors. The hardware changes will be physiological and anatomical. The overall efficiency of the nervous system will be increased by improvements in its component parts and changes in size and in muscle bulk have consequences in terms of strength and speed of movement. In addition to these obviously biological factors the manner in which the hardware is utilised or programmed by software (the more psychological variables such as task analysis, the refinement of action plans and the availability of highly practised sub-routines) will have a profound effect on the nature and quality of the skills that the individual has available. In writing a computer programme the experienced programmer will produce one which requires the minimum number of operations and thus achieves the desired end in the shortest running time and with the greatest economy. In contrast the less experienced programmer, particularly if the operations required are complex, is likely to include some redundant or less economical routines.

Hands and tools

The human hand is a remarkable instrument of human intelligence and a powerful agent of the mind. It is probably the most elegant and skilful organ that has ever been developed through natural selection and paradoxically it is specialised to be unspecialised. The hand is used for many purposes, such as pulling, pushing, poking, scratching, but primarily it is a grasping or prehensile organ showing a vast range of purposive actions rather than a multiplicity of movements. A limited range of movements is harnessed to the production of a great array of purposive acts. A basic requirement of prehension is that an object should be grasped securely, irrespective of its properties or the purpose to which it is to be put. Stability is essential for any subsequent activity no matter what the intention, whether it is to move a heavy object or carry out fine manipulation. Stability is not necessarily related to force or power and it is characteristic that the adult human can hold securely in his hand a heavy stone or a delicate object like a butterfly or a fine glass vial. Tools of all kinds—pencils, brushes, cutlery, screwdrivers and so on—make up a special and important class of objects.

Man is not the only animal to use tools. The burrowing wasp is known to use a tiny pebble as a hammer to pound the soil down over its nest of eggs and finches have been observed using a cactus spine to pick insects from crevices in a tree trunk. Almost two hundred years ago Benjamin Franklin wrote 'Man is a tool making animal.' In this he is not unique: Jane Goodall has described Chimpanzees fashioning a simple tool by trimming a blade of sword grass with which to 'fish' in termite nests. The differences between men and apes in respect of tool using is not simply a reflection of the mind which provides the idea or the plan. The anatomy of the hand differs between apes and men and certain properties of the human hand are fundamental to human manual skill. The ability to oppose the pulp surfaces of the thumb and fingers is necessary for fine dextrous movements as is the ability to converge and diverge the fingers and move them independently of each other.

The development of tool using

Grasping can be seen in the newborn baby. If a finger is pressed gently into a baby's palm then his fingers will synergistically curl around it in what is called a reflex grasp. It is reflex because it occurs only in response to a certain kind of tactual stimulus, but the mechanism is nevertheless complicated and not fully understood. Gradually over the first six months or so of the first year the reflex grasp gives way to visually directed reaching. Reaching of this kind, which as its name implies is usually to a visual target, is not stimulus-bound in the way that the reflex grasp is.

The emergence of visually directed reaching is gradual via a number of stages which have been charted in detail by B. L. White and his colleagues in Cambridge, Massachusetts. These workers also showed that the rate at which visually directed reaching develops can be markedly affected by the child's experiences and exposure to suitable stimulation. In the second half of the first year the baby begins to use his hands much more. He swipes at objects in his visual field, reaches out to them and captures them. He exchanges objects between his hands, bangs them, grasps them and laboriously releases them. Somewhere towards the end of his first year the infant is likely to have his first exposure to tools. The ability to use a tool, no matter how crudely, is a big step in a child's development. It implies conceptual thought and the power of abstraction, the ability to visualise the relationship between objects and goals. It is in fact a reflection of the child's developing intelligence and problem-solving capacity as he begins to exert control over his environment.

Along with one of my students, Mary Dalgleish, I have recently begun to study the development of the use of tools in infancy. So far our studies are in the early stages and we have concentrated on examining the changes in grip-patterns which the child exhibits. Mothers often give their babies a spoon to play with at meal times and of course the baby begins to experiment with the feeding process. Between ten and twelve months, grips assumed on the spoon vary a good deal and often they are singularly inappropriate to the task of coping with a bowl of cereal. Some of the grip patterns which we have observed are shown in Figure 4. The way the tool is held

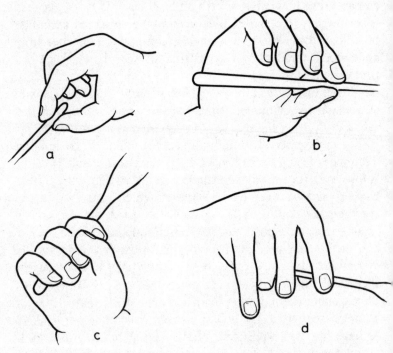

Figure 4   Grip positions used by infants between ten and eighteen months.

imposes great constraints on what can be done with it. It is, for example, virtually impossible to transfer food to the mouth if the spoon is held by the grips shown in Figure 4a or 4b, where the control and facility for adjustment is very limited. Gradually over a period of a few months the baby refines a grasp-pattern similar to those shown in Figure 4c and 4d which do permit the transfer of food. With practice, which of course occurs several times a day, the reliance upon one pattern increases and the less useful grips drop out. We believe that we are witnessing the appearance of a sub-routine which is gradually becoming modularised. As the sub-routine is practised and refined, not only can the child utilise it with increasing confidence and reliability but also it requires less of his attention to monitor it. Thus as his processing capacity is freed from monitoring this component he is able to devote more of his attention to other parts of the task and to refining the programme as a whole.

As I said above the hand displays a vast range of purposive actions rather than a multiplicity of movements. The adult appears to possess a number of modular sub-routines which can be linked together in order to perform any number of different actions. In this way an analogy can be drawn between skills and language. Given a number of words, these can be combined in a variety of ways according to grammatical rules so as to generate a large array of utterances, many of which will be novel to the individual.

Along with studies on the development of sub-routines it is necessary also to examine how programmes of action are constructed and controlled. One traditional technique in biology is to insert a perturbation into a system and study its effects. Here the kind of thing I have in mind is to alter the properties of the tool and study how the child adapts to this. One might, for example, give a child a specially constructed spoon where the balance is altered so that to control it adequately it must be grasped in a different way. Another approach to studying the construction of action programmes is to examine how the two hands are used in complementary roles to achieve certain ends. Picking up a peg and locating it in a hole is a task having the properties of a skilled action but it is a task accomplished with one hand. In contrast to this, threading beads on a lace is a task requiring the use of both hands in which each hand carries out different functions, one holding the bead and the other locating the lace in the hole. Interestingly, in the execution of this task the hands reverse roles. When the lace has been located that hand, say the right, then holds the bead whilst the left pulls the lace through. In previous observations on children carrying out tasks such as this one we have found that when they are asked to use their non-preferred hand there is a tendency for a child to revert to a less dextrous power-grip configuration, whereas for exactly the same task the preferred hand makes use of a precision grip.

Paradoxically, development can be seen as reducing the available options. A relatively large repertoire of grip-patterns is exchanged for the ready availability of a smaller number of reliable ones. Flexibility, an important characteristic of skilled behaviour, is not lost by this process; it is achieved in other ways. Quite a small number of reliable and precise sub-routines are deployed by a rich motor syntax into a very large array of action programmes.

Skill, then, is a process of construction whereby the individual achieves certain ends and thus exerts control over aspects of the environment. Such creative activity has obvious similarities to other cognitive activities, to problem solving, concept formation and aspects of perception. The manner in which components are mastered and then linked together in various ways, gradually giving rise to increasingly complex motor skills, may well have implications for educational theory and practice.

Children's inferences
PETER BRYANT

The typical adult's understanding of the world around him is imperfect in many ways. Yet this understanding is always a great deal better than it was when he was a young child. Young children (about five years old) are often quite plainly confused when they have to deal with such basic notions as number, quantity, space and time, and confused in situations which create no problems at all for an adult. That children have relative difficulties in understanding what is going on around them has been the main point of most of the work on cognitive development which has been done over the last thirty years or so. It is an extremely important point, because it immediately raises the question of whether there are some things that young children are quite incapable of grasping. If there are, then we have information which has practical, educational value as well as theoretical significance; for why should one bother trying to teach a young child something which he simply will not be able to learn? Surely it is more efficient, and less frustrating to child and teacher alike, to wait until they are both on the same wavelength.

Perhaps it is the obvious force of this argument which has spurred psychologists to build up an extraordinarily bleak picture of the young child's capabilities, a picture which seems to have been accepted without criticism by many educators. Experiment after experiment has apparently demonstrated that the young child of four and five years or thereabouts lacks some very basic logical abilities which are essential to the proper understanding of many of the things which happen to him.

One example of inference
There are now some signs—from my own work and that of other researchers—that this enthusiastic pessimism about young children might well have gone too far, and that many of these

experiments have some remarkable weaknesses. Here I shall concentrate on one significant example. This concerns inferences of the sort which involve combining two items of information in order to make a completely new judgment. Many psychologists have claimed that children younger than seven years or so are quite incapable of managing such an inference. This is indeed a serious claim, since someone who is unable to put together the memories which he has from separate experiences will surely be able to learn very little from his environment.

One attempt to show that young children cannot manage this sort of inference was made by two American psychologists, Howard and Tracy Kendler. They constructed a task in which children of various ages were given three boxes standing side by side. They learned that making an appropriate response such as pressing a handle to each of the two side boxes produced a glass or a steel marble. These were called *sub-goals* and the children had to learn that one of the two side boxes produced the glass marble and the other the steel one.

Then in a separate stage they learned that inserting one of these sub-goals, but not the other, through the hole in the centre box, produced a reward such as a toy, which the Kendlers called the *major goal*. Once the children had learned both which side box produced which sub-goal and also which sub-goal produced the major goal, they were told to set about getting the major goal for themselves. The question was whether they would be able straight away first to obtain the right sub-goal and then to use it to produce the major goal.

Five-year-old children showed no sign of being able to do this. Nor were eight-year-olds much better. In fact only adults solved this task consistently well. Does this mean that children cannot combine separate experiences inferentially? There are grounds for hesitation here. For example, one group of experimenters repeated the Kendlers' experiment with rural Liberian children and adults. Adults as well as children found the task very difficult. However these experimenters also noticed that their Liberian helpers were usually bemused and often extremely frightened by this strange problem and the unusual gadgetry which it involved, so they carried out another similar sort of experiment which involved familiar material such as matchboxes and keys and this change considerably improved the performance of the people they were studying. This effect is not confined to Liberians, since a colleague of mine at Oxford, Simon Kewson, has recently shown that children as young as three and four years who fail in the task devised by the Kendlers nonetheless succeed when the material used is more familiar to them (oranges in drawers, for instance). These young children *can* combine separate experiences.

The wider implications and Piaget

There is a certain knockabout quality to the experiments which I have described so far, and I think that it is fair to say that they have not had a great impact outside the area of psychology. This rider does not apply to the work of Piaget who has also argued that young children cannot make some kinds of inference. His work is taken very seriously indeed by a wide variety of people, including many who work in the field of education.

Piaget suggests that young children are in many ways illogical and only acquire their logical abilities very gradually. His observations cover a wide range of behaviour. As far as inferences are concerned he has concentrated on transitive inferences. We adults know that A is greater than C whenever A is greater than B and B is greater than C. Piaget claims that young children do not know this, and the kind of observation which led him to this conclusion is neatly described in the following quotation from a recent book of his:

'We present two sticks to a child, stick A being smaller than stick B. Then we hide stick A and show him stick B together with a larger stick C. Then we ask him how A and C compare. Pre-operational children [those below seven years] will say that they do not know because they have not seen them together — they have not been able to compare them.'

This sort of observation has been repeated many times, by Piaget and others, and at first sight it seems to show that young children cannot combine separate items of information along a continuum inferentially.

Now if a child cannot manage this particular kind of inference he is unlikely to be able to measure or to understand the process of measurement, since using a ruler must involve combining separate judgments about quantity. So we need to look at the traditional experiment on transitive inferences very carefully, and further inspection shows that it does have a number of serious weaknesses.

One of these is that the child who fails may be quite capable of combining the two original direct comparisons, A is greater than B and B is greater than C, but may simply have forgotten them at the time that he is asked the inferential question. There is a simple way of clearing up this uncertainty, and that is to test the child's memory for the direct comparisons at the same time as asking him to combine them inferentially. Only if he remembers the direct comparisons but cannot put them together to make the inference, is it possible to conclude that he cannot produce a logical inference.

The omission of this basic precaution is not the only thing wrong with the traditional transitivity experiment. It is also possible that the older children of eight years and above who normally solve the problem correctly may be doing so without going through the genuinely inferential process of combining A and C through B. They may instead be 'parrotting'. The problem is that in the original direct comparisons AB and BC, A is the larger and C the smaller. Yet the correct answer to A in the inferential AC question is 'larger' and to C 'smaller'. It follows that the child might answer this question correctly merely by repeating a verbal label picked up in the initial comparisons without actually making an inference at all.

Again there is a simple control, which is to increase the number of quantities involved. Suppose there are five quantities such that A is greater than B, which is greater than C, and so on down to E. Then one could have four initial direct comparisons A is greater than B, B is greater then C, C is greater than D, and D is greater than E. Note that three of these quantities, B,C,D, crop up in two of the comparisons, and each is in one comparison the smaller and in the other the larger. Thus any new inferential comparisons based just on these three quantities could not be solved by parrotting since each of them would have been equally often larger and smaller in the initial comparisons. In fact there is only one new indirect inferential comparison which can be based on these three quantities and this is between B and D.

An inference experiment with controls

When in 1969 my colleague Tom Trabasso and I began to work on this problem we could find no study in the vast literature which existed on it which had included both these essential controls. So we conducted a series of experiments, one of which can be described here very briefly. In it we showed children of four and five years five rods of different colours, A, B, C, D, and E. They saw only the tips of each of these rods, but we taught them quite thoroughly that A was longer than B, B than C, C than D, and D than E. Thus we made sure that they would be likely to remember the original comparisons. Once they knew these four direct comparisons we passed on to the second stage of the experiment in which we tested their memory for these original direct comparisons and their ability to combine them inferentially. The crucial question was whether they would be able to make the BD inference.

In fact both four- and five-year-old children not only remembered the direct comparisons which they had been taught but did also make the BD inference correctly over eighty per cent of the time. This result has now been repeated many times by different investigators with substantially the same results.

However, even this conclusion can be criticised. Recently it has been suggested that the children might simply have associated B with the largest endpoint A and D with the smallest endpoint E, and concluded from these associations that B is larger than D. This would not be transitive inference which must involve associating B and D through their relations to the common C. However we have effectively ruled out this alternative in an experiment in which B and D are as usual associated with their respective endpoints, but are not connected through the middle C. In this situation, where they cannot make an inference, children do not conclude that B is larger than D.

My conclusion, on balance, is that young children can make transitive inferences rather well, provided that they can remember the information they are required to combine, and that the general pessimism about their ability to combine separate experiences is almost certainly ill-founded. It may be that many of the other, similarly pessimistic, claims that have been made about young children's abilities should also be looked at with some care. It is very easy to lead a young child into making mistakes in an experiment for one reason or another. Doing him justice often needs much more care.

However, now that we have cleared up some problems about the transitivity experiment, we are still faced with questions about real life. The young child makes inferences in formal, austere and relatively simple experimental conditions, but does he also make them in his normal surroundings, the home and the school?

One possibility is that he makes them about everyday perceptual information. Children, for example, often find it difficult to remember the orientation of figures in their environment. Yet we have shown that these difficulties often disappear if these figures parallel some constant feature of the background. Surely this is an inference, since the child must be working out that two figures, seen successively, were in the same orientation because they were both in the same orientation as something else. If A and B both parallel C, then A parallels B.

If this is so, inferences may be a basic tool with which the child organises and understands his informal perceptual experiences from a very early age. But this still leaves us with the more formal tasks which the child has to deal with when he goes to school. One such task is measuring. But measuring, though it depends on an inference, also involves something else.

A child who uses a ruler to compare two things must be able not only to make a transitive inference, as I have shown above, but also to gather the information necessary for the inference. He must know not only that $A=C$ when $A=B$ and $B=C$, but also that in order to compare A and C inferentially he must find his ruler, B, and take it to A and C.

At the moment our research suggests that young children are rather bad in active inferential tasks. We have taken children who perform perfectly well when all the information needed for an inference is handed to them, so to speak, on a plate. Yet these same children managed abysmally when we asked them how two quantities (A and C), which could not be perceived together, compared. In this task we gave them a third stick, B, with which they could have solved the problem but they simply did not use it. They could make inferences, but they seemed to have difficulty in spontaneously gathering the information on which an inference could be based.

Perhaps this result tells us something about the educational needs of the young child. It may be that we ought to take the line that children should be shown how to take advantage of the logical abilities which they already have. They should be shown, perhaps, how to make these abilities effective. My own opinion is that this is a much better course than just assuming that young children are not logical and passively waiting for logical development to take place.

SEX DIFFERENCES IN BEHAVIOUR

Few people dispute that there are differences in the behaviour of males and females. The question at issue is, what are the origins of these differences? Are they rooted in truly specific biological characteristics? Or does social custom generate definable sex roles? Experiments on animals and observations on humans go some way to resolving these problems. Nevertheless, interpretations of the experimental data sometimes diverge, producing one of the most controversial areas of developmental psychology in humans.

Sex Differences: biology and behaviour
CORINNE HUTT

In the human, distinctively male and female development begins soon after conception. From birth, cultural and social pressures act upon an organism which already has certain predispositions and propensities resulting from early hormonal influences. Biology and culture therefore are different aspects of a continuous process of interaction—they are not processes which in themselves are in opposition to each other. To acknowledge the biological bases of such predispositions contributes to a proper understanding of how, in the process of becoming boy or girl, man or woman, an individual is constrained in certain ways, primed in others, and how he or she develops certain aptitudes and skills and how these are related to the individual's role in society. In other words, the manner in which the social environment may accentuate or attenuate differences between individuals can only be evaluated in relation to the bases upon which such influences are operating.

Sexual dimorphism characterises all mammalian species and is principally associated with reproductive roles. In humans, no less than in other mammals, these structurally dimorphic features would be curious anomalies were they not accompanied by some behavioural and psychological differences. In mammals the active process of sexual differentiation is that of the male. In the presence of the Y-chromosome (the 'male' chromosome) the embryonic gonad differentiates into a testis (in the seventh week of pregnancy in humans). The hormone secreted by the foetal testis then organises internal tract and genitalia into the male form and finally acts upon the brain to organise it according to the male pattern. Female differentiation is not a similarly active process—it simply occurs in the *absence* of the male hormone.

There are three characteristics which seem to be inherent in masculine development. First, the male is more vulnerable and more at risk for a variety of disorders: more male than female foetuses are aborted, the male infant is more susceptible to a variety of perinatal and postnatal complications and throughout life men remain more at risk for many diseases and accidents. With improvements in conditions and services over the years, the expectation of life for both sexes has increased, but considerably more for women than for men. In the last 130 years for instance, the expectation of life for a man at seventy years has increased by one month while for a woman it has increased by sixteen months. Nor is this vulnerability confined to the physical aspects of development: mental retardation is more common in males and so are a number of disorders like autism, speech defects, reading disabilities, visual and hearing defects and behaviour disturbances. Truancy, delinquency and referrals to Child Guidance Clinics are also far more common amongst boys than amongst girls.

Second, a greater variety of phenotypes characterises males. That is, in the expression of characters which are continuously distributed in a population, more males than females are represented at the extremes of the distribution. Thus, while there is little evidence that men and women differ in average intelligence, both very high and very low IQs are more frequently found amongst men. Even with a highly selected sample such as students graduating from Keele in the period 1953 to 1972, this trend is discernible (see Figure 1).

Growth differences

Some of the phenomena attributed to the greater vulnerability of the male are really a consequence of this greater phenotypic variety. Even where no physical causes can be ascertained, as in delinquency, then, by virtue of the statistical generalisation formulated in the last paragraph, more males than females are found in such a category. By the same token, if the antithesis to delinquency could be agreed upon (saintliness?) one would expect to find more men in such a category too.

Third, males are more retarded in their development despite the fact that sexual differentiation is completed earlier. Speed of growth in the boy lags about two years behind the girl's and bone ossification is completed later, while puberty is attained

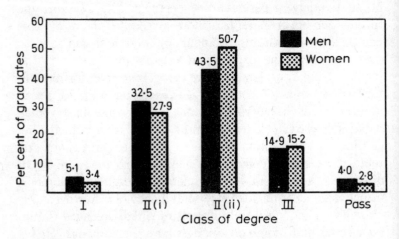

Figure 1   Sex difference in class of degrees obtained by students at Keele University.

roughly two and a half years later (see Figure 2). Boys are also retarded in many aspects of behavioural development. Girls tend to sit, crawl and walk earlier than boys; they acquire language earlier and their proficiency in a number of intellectual skills is attained well before boys. This relatively accelerated development of girls is now known to be under the control of the female hormones. When oestrogens are administered to rats during critical periods of the development of the central nervous system they produce precocious brain maturation.

The oestrogen effect on brain maturation, however, may be only one of the processes accounting for the disparity between the rates of development of the two sexes. In 1959 J. M. Tanner *et al* suggested that the Y-chromosome itself may be implicated in the control of the rate of development. More recently (in 1972) C. Ounsted and D. C. Taylor put forward a theory concerning the role of the Y-chromosome which accounts for the three characteristics just discussed. Their theory, briefly, states that the Y-chromosome, though carrying no genetic information itself, nevertheless elicits more information from the genome (the whole gene library); this increased genetic 'read-out' is made possible by the slower development of the male and allows greater phenotypic variety.

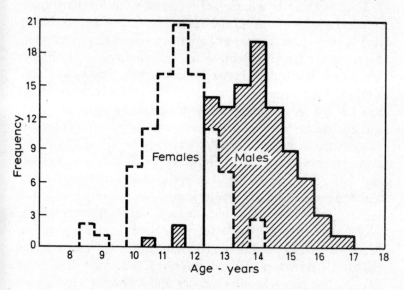

Figure 2   The histogram shows the periods of maximum growth in males and females.

If more genetic information is expressed in the male, it follows that more disadvantageous as well as more beneficial traits will be manifest—hence the predominance of males at the extremes of a distribution.

If development is protracted, it follows that periods of risk and critical or sensitive periods in boys are extended. Thus both benign and malign influences are allowed more time to operate. This fact would also contribute to the greater variance and inconsistency observed in males. As part of a longitudinal study of over a thousand children in a Swedish town, Lars Bergman of the University of Stockholm analysed the intellectual performance of boys and girls who, between the ages of ten and thirteen years, had missed long periods of school due to illness or had experienced some domestic upheaval. These adverse circumstances were found to depress the performance of boys, particularly in non-verbal areas. The performance of girls remained relatively unimpaired.

Despite their developmental retardation, males have many physical advantages from the outset. At birth they are larger, they develop proportionately larger hearts and lungs and hence have greater stroke volume and vital capacity. From birth to senesence their calory intake is greater and they have a consistently higher basal metabolism. Since the male body has less fat and more muscle per unit volume, its inertia will be less and hence speed of movement will be greater. Moreover, the greater length and smaller 'carrying angle' of the male's arm ensure greater velocity and precision in hitting and throwing skills. Such differences equip the male for a more active and strenuous life, the evolutionary advantage of which is self-evident. They may also help to explain some of the exuberance and physical activity of boys. In a study of the leisure activities of children, my colleagues Jill Newton and Barbara Rand asked six- and seven-year-olds what they most liked doing at weekends outdoors and indoors—what games they liked playing, who their playmates were, and to name their best friend and favourite toy. Over 72 per cent of the boys, in contrast to 34 per cent of the girls, preferred an active physical pursuit, and while the girls were as likely to choose physical activity as fantasy-play outdoors, boys showed an unambiguous preference for physical play. Even indoors, where conditions would normally militate against such activity, nearly one quarter of boys nevertheless chose some physical pursuit. It is hardly surprising that many nursery schools have a preponderance of boys on their waiting lists!

With regard to choice of playmates, boys and girls most frequently preferred children of their own sex but a few liked playing with both; no girls chose a boy as their playmate, though one boy chose a girl. Boys and girls also had children of their own sex as best friends, though a few more girls than boys had an opposite-sex friend—perhaps a precocious manifestation of adolescent interests! Boys mostly preferred mechanical toys and girls preferred dolls, though the preferences of the girls were less exclusive than those of boys.

Boys and girls also differ in certain sensory and perceptual capacities, the differences often being evident soon after birth. Girls have lower touch and pain thresholds, a keener sense of smell, are better at sound discrimination and localisation. Boys on the other hand have superior visual and spatial abilities. The early reliance on particular sensory modalities has special implications for learning and education. In a study of the effect of the modality in which information was presented upon the recall and recognition memory of girls and boys of different ages, we found that girls were superior to boys in both types of memory, whichever the modality. But the female superiority was more true of nine-year-olds than of sixteen-year-olds. More interestingly, the boys were at their greatest disadvantage when the information was presented in the auditory modality. Visual presentation of stimuli, on the other hand, minimised the sex differences: it appeared that whatever advantage the boys may have had in the visual modality was countered by the overall superiority of the girls.

From a very early age boys and girls begin to develop rather different life-styles. The foundations of these clearly lie in certain predispositions, sensory capacities, and behavioural differences which are under a measure of genetic control. But the characteristic styles develop because of the reinforcement the individuals receive from these various endeavours, because they receive support or discouragement from influential adults and their peers, and because these generalise to other spheres of activity.

In several recent studies of over two hundred nursery school children we found that the origins of these life-styles were evident even at the age of three and four years. Boys were more active and energetic, more exploratory, more 'thing-orientated' and more effective with the inanimate. Girls were more affiliative and 'person-orientated', more easily inhibited by novelty or uncertainty; they tended to construe personal relationships and social situations in a more complex manner and differentiate more subtly along social and emotional dimensions.

Hormones and aggression

Boys, we found, were twice as aggressive as girls, both physically and verbally. But not only did they *display* more aggression, they also *elicited* it more frequently. There are other attributes like assertiveness, competitiveness and ambition which have some affinity to aggression but are less disruptive. Evidence to date suggests that all these features are to some extent influenced by the action of the male hormone.

Many of these sex-typical patterns of behaviour are shared by several primate species and clearly have their origins in the hormonally-controlled masculinisation or feminisation of the foetal brain. There are three quite distinct sources of evidence which substantiate this case. The first source consists of the results obtained in the 1960s by Harry Harlow from animals which were reared with dummy surrogates during the first few weeks of life. Nevertheless, from about three months of age these animals exhibited the sex-typical patterns of threat, rough-and-tumble play, grooming etcetera with near-normal frequency.

The second source lies in studies of hormonal manipulation of the sexual differentiation of the brain. When androgens are administered to a pregnant monkey, any genetic female foetus is masculinised and subsequently shows levels of threat, chasing and rough-and-tumble play, comparable with those of normal genetic males. Conversely, the administration of anti-androgens which inhibit the action of the male hormone, has a feminising effect both upon morphology and upon behaviour, reducing aggression and physical activity.

The third source concerns the human analogues of these animal experiments, namely the sexual anomalies which result from 'natural' accidents. Genetic females exposed *in utero* to excess androgens secreted from the adrenals due to metabolic disorder, subsequently manifested 'boyish' interests: they showed a preference for physical activities and boys' toys, were generally described as tomboys, had little interest in marriage and child-care but were keen on pursuing a career. Boys who were similarly exposed to excess androgen *in utero* were found to be more physically vigorous and aggressive than their brothers.

Conversely, cases of testicular feminisation (genetic males who are phenotypic females due to the ineffectiveness of their sex hormones) showed predominantly feminine interests. Moreover, very recently it has been found that boys whose diabetic mothers had been treated with female hormones while bearing them, were less aggressive, less assertive, had poorer athletic skill and spatial ability than both normal controls and the sons of diabetic mothers who had not been treated with female hormones.

The fact that such sex-typical characteristics are under a measure of genetic control means that during evolution they must have conferred some selective advantage. In hunter-gatherer societies where the males roam far and wide while the females nurture their young in the home, the advantage of the dimorphism in sensory and behavioural propensities is only too obvious. What is less clear, however, is the selective advantage to be gained by females by their superiority in language. It is difficult to see why any benefits that may have accrued to women would not also have been advantageous to men. It seems to me, however, that the superiority in language may more plausibly be regarded as an inevitable consequence of the precocious development of the female. Since brain maturation, and hence lateralisation of function, occurs earlier in the female, those centres concerned with the control of language are functional earlier. Once proficiency in language has been acquired, reliance on other skills is pre-empted to a certain extent. Language is generally the most economical vehicle for the acquisition and dissemination of information.

Language and social interactions

These developmental differences have a number of educational implications. During the preschool period for instance, girls are passing through proportionately more of the formative

period than are boys. Consequently the time during which
the girl is concerned with active exploration of her environment, and during which she is able to lay down the manipulative, operational, and non-linguistic bases upon which to
consolidate more complex cognitive skills, is foreshortened,
and it may be necessary to compensate for this. Again, the fact
that girls of three and four, as we found, spend almost twenty-
five per cent of their time in social interactions, usually of a
verbal kind, emphasises their need for stimulating dialogue.

Sex differences, it is often said, are the results of society's
attempts to perpetuate sex-stereotypes. They result from
society's expectations and values. Such an argument, however,
is irrefutable and therefore scientifically sterile. Nevertheless,
it is notable that even in those societies which have strenuously
endeavoured to eliminate traditional sex roles, dimorphism
in function and interests still persists.

The social-induction argument also begs the question: on
what basis would such expectations be formulated? Are we
to assume, for instance, that all societies make an *a priori* de-
claration that aggression is to be tolerated in males but not in
females? Social systems cannot fashion or create such models
anew—they may modify, accentuate or attenuate the biological
propensities already extant. In other words, it is the predisposition itself which forms the basis for social expectations
and which may be amplified thereby. It is only by acknowledging these predispositions that we can help individuals fulfil
their potential.

Sex Differences : biological and social interaction
JOHN ARCHER & BARBARA LLOYD

Profound changes in our understanding of the nature of behavioural sex differences have taken place in the last hundred
years. Freud challenged the notion that masculinity and fem-
ininity were divinely ordained and explained sex role development in terms of identification. Basically his approach was
mechanistic and he believed that biology was destiny. The
Freudian view of the universality of the oedipal complex was
quickly challenged by anthropologists eager to demonstrate
that the family dynamics which Freud described were limited
to the middle-class Viennese milieu which he and his patients
shared. Ambivalence towards the father was questioned by
Bronislaw Malinowski's studies in the Trobriand Islands;
the turbulence of puberty and adolescence was disputed from
Margaret Mead's Samoan experience, and her later researches
in New Guinea led to the assertion that the most fundamental
aspects of male and female temperament were culturally
conditioned.

A division in interpretation

Psychologists measured affective behaviour and intellectual
functioning and produced systematic, quantitative evidence
of male-female differences for which cultural learning explanations were often offered. In the 1950s the heated heredity-
environment controversies of earlier decades appeared to be
resolved by a general recognition that neither biological nor
cultural explanations were adequate in themselves to explain
development. Nonetheless classic studies such as Jerome Kagan
and Howard Moss' longitudinal analysis of aggression, dependence, independence and achievement relied heavily on
learning to account for the failure to find predictive value in
early measures of dependence in boys and aggression in girls.
The necessity to learn adult norms of sex-appropriate behaviour

was invoked to account for discontinuities in development, and biological factors were merely mentioned speculatively. A socialisation account was similarly central to the theory which Herman Witkin and his colleagues proposed to explain differences in cognitive style. Towards the end of the 1960s there appeared renewed attempts to explain these same differences from a biological perspective, the first of these being Donald Broverman and co-authors' theory of hormonally-produced differences in activation and inhibition in the central nervous system. Thus, although concensus emerged on the need to consider both biological and social variables to account for the development of sex differences, explanatory arguments still leaned on one or the other set of variables.

The interactionist approach

Clearly, a more complex model which gives more equal weight to both sources of influence is required. An interactionist approach describes the effort to account for the complex relationship between biological and social factors which occurs as the result of repeated feedback by their action and reaction on one another. In considering genetic and environmental influences on behaviour an interactionist interpretation would view the genotype as providing a flexible plan, but not a fixed blueprint, for the developmental process. The final outcome would be determined by interaction with environmental conditions prevailing at each successive moment in the process. Thus to ask whether behaviour is determined by the genotype or environmental conditions is no longer meaningful, and investigation shifts to considering how the genetic basis of behaviour is expressed in a range of environmental conditions.

The interactionist model is complex and may fail to produce an easily comprehensible explanation. Instead, a popular approach has been to acknowledge the importance of both social and biological factors but to draw upon the explanatory power of one while virtually ignoring the other. Following this pattern has been the recent resurgence of biological interpretations of sex differences, which probably reflects the major advances which have been made in the genetics and endocrinology of sexual differentiation. Typical of these is Corrine Hutt's chapter (see page 158). She begins by acknowledging that 'Biology and culture are different aspects of a continuous process of interaction. . .' and proposes an additive model in which 'the social environment may accentuate or attenuate differences between individuals'.

In our discussion we shall attempt to identify and clarify the issues which make an interactionist explanation difficult both for the theorist and researcher to maintain consistently. In seeking to understand the difficulties encountered, it is useful to consider both the content and the structure of the interactionist model. By content we refer to the different scientific disciplines which must contribute to the analysis, while the structure refers to the formal relationships between the variables.

Content: an interdisciplinary enterprise

An understanding of the aetiology of sex differences which takes account of both biological and social factors must be an interdisciplinary enterprise. Data and theory might be drawn from genetics, physiology, endocrinology, animal behaviour, psychology, anthropology or sociology. No single researcher can be expected to have had training and experience encompassing such a variety of sciences. One solution is for investigators to work in multidisciplinary teams: the internationally known experts on human sexuality, Masters and Johnson, are a physician and social psychologist respectively. Although less renowned, Nicholas Blurton-Jones and M. J. Konner, ethologist and anthropologist, have contributed significantly to our understanding of the development of sex differences. Team research can supply some of the answers, but it is still worth considering the special problems involved when the social scientist employs biological findings, and the biologist uses the results from the social sciences.

Laymen and professional biologists alike agree that tremendous advances have been made in biochemistry, genetics and endocrinology in recent years. For example, the presence of the Barr body in a slide of cells taken from a simple smear of buccal tissue allows positive identification of a genetic female; testosterone administered before a female rat is four days old prevents oestrous cycling at maturity even with hormone replacement in adulthood. It is hardly surprising that the psychologist or anthropologist is struck by the apparent certainty which biological research produces. In an epistemological sense the data with which the biological scientist works offers material reality while their own behavioural variables are difficult to specify and measure and may appear by comparison as epiphenomena. Perhaps it is this appearance of material reality which makes explanations of sex differences primarily in terms of the biological sciences so attractive.

Even when biological evidence is drawn from behavioural studies there are pitfalls for the social scientist to overcome. Data which are drawn from observations on animals are frequently interpreted in terms of concepts derived from human behaviour (aggression, fear, and dominance, for example). By applying a common label to behavioural results from animal and human subjects, the inference that there is a causal similarity between the two sets of data can become an unquestioned starting point for further theorising. The apparent close correspondence between animal and human sex differences in aggression obscures diversity in the observational basis of the comparison: the animal findings rely on measures of initial attack, threat displays, or duration and outcome of fighting, whereas the human evidence includes teachers' ratings of assertiveness, self-evaluation on questionnaires and willingness to administer strong electric shocks to peers in a laboratory setting.

The biological scientist who turns to social science data is generally unimpressed by the explanatory power of the theories he encounters. Thus the anthropologist's view that differences in behaviour reflect different positions of the sexes in the social structure, or the sociologist's interpretation of similar behavioural data as reflecting group pressures or power relationships, may be ignored by the biologist. A flagrant example of this sort of treatment is Desmond Morris's handling of cross-cultural information in his book *The Naked Ape*. In arguing against the use of anthropological findings he asserts: 'the simple tribal groups that are living today are not primitive, they are stultified. Truly primitive tribes have not existed for thousands of years. The naked ape is essentially an exploratory species and any society that has failed to advance has in some sense failed, "gone wrong".'

A further potential source of difficulty in using psychological or sociological material lies in a tendency to accept concepts in terms of their face validity, perhaps even to reify them. Thus on the one hand the cognitive style which Herman Witkin has identified as more frequent in males is labelled 'field independence' while that characterising females is called 'field dependence'. It is a simple matter to forget that the measures from which these labels are inferred involve either the search for a simple line-drawn pattern in a more complex presentation or the ability to adjust a rod to the true vertical or horizontal despite a misleading frame. How different the female trait would have appeared had Witkin and his colleagues chosen to label it 'field sensitivity'!

Structure: a feedback of influences

Central to an understanding of an interactionist model is the concept of feedback. In this section, we discuss first the simple form of feedback loop which is useful in understanding the two-way nature of hormonal influences on behaviour. We then go on to show how a series of interrelated feedback loops extended in time can illustrate features of the interaction between organism and environment in development.

When discussing sex hormones we have to consider not only how they affect behaviour, but how behaviour affects the hormones. The large number of studies showing influences in the former direction have been drawn upon extensively in biologically based theories of sex differences, whereas those showing the influence of behaviour on hormones are seldom remarked upon. There is, however, increasing evidence that such influences are important. Thus, R. M. Rose and his co-workers found that defeat of a male rhesus monkey by another male led to a rapid and pronounced fall in plasma testosterone levels, showing that not only does the male hormone influence aggression but that the outcome of aggressive encounters influences the male hormone levels. Another aspect of Rose's work was concerned with the influence of sexual behaviour on hormonal levels in male monkeys. He found that a two or threefold increase in testosterone occurred when males were given access to a receptive female. Similarly, K. Purvis and N. B. Haynes have found a rise in testosterone levels in male rats provided with receptive partners, in this case beginning even before tactile contact.

Social environment can also influence female sex hormones. Synchronisation of menstrual cycles was investigated by M. K. McClintock in an all-women's college: she found increasing synchrony in women who spent most time together and longer cycles for women having little contact with men. Contact with the opposite sex led to a shortening of these cycles.

Stress is known to decrease both male and female sex hormone levels. John Mason and his colleagues found that both sexes of rhesus monkey showed considerably lowered hormone levels when undergoing prolonged sessions in which they had to press a lever repeatedly to avoid electric shock. Similar examples are found in research on humans, Rose and his co-workers reporting a dramatic lowering of testosterone levels in soldiers undergoing basic training for the Vietnam War.

We have used research on behaviour and sex hormones to illustrate one important component of the interactionist model, that there is a two-way and not a one-way influence between the variables. Figure 1 summarises the position diagramma-tically, contrasting this feedback loop with a simpler one which recognises sex hormone effects on behaviour but not the reverse.

The feedback loop is also applicable to the relationship

between physical characteristics and the social environment. Behaviour can be influenced indirectly by the way in which the individual appears to others in the social group. Peter Marler found that by painting the breast of a female chaffinch red, males would treat the female as if she were a male, and subsequently her behaviour changed accordingly so that she became as aggressive as males.

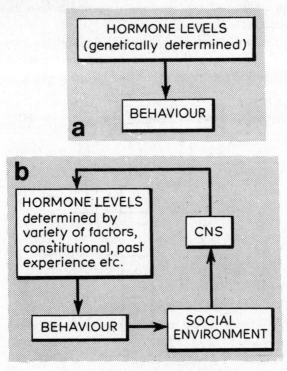

Figure 1:
(a)   Simple model of hormonal-behavioural relationships.
(b)   Interactionist model of hormonal-behavioural relationships.

So far we have discussed how social and biological influences produce mutual reactions which can be represented by a simple feedback model. These interactions are of a relatively restricted nature and cover short periods of time. To appreciate fully the complexity of interactions which are involved in the aetiology of sex differences we must view development as a series of such simple feedbacks but involving more complex features and being greatly extended in time. Thus a continuous series of feedbacks between the organism and its environment throughout life is envisaged. Psychologists may find it difficult to make this extension in time because of the reliance on cross sectional data for testing theories of development when longitudinal or limited experimental data might have been more appropriate.

Figure 2a illustrates the interactive model, in diagrammatic form, showing how the organism and its environment continually influence one another in a two-way process of action

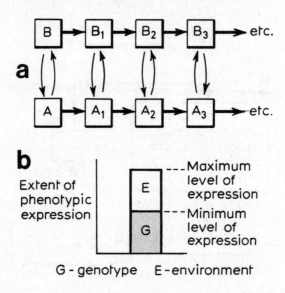

Figure 2:
(a) Interactive model of genotype-environment interaction.
(b) Simple (additive) model of genotype-environment interactions.

and reaction. $A \rightarrow A_n$ and $B \rightarrow B_n$ represent the organism and environment at each successive stage of the interaction. A and B are the initial states, which are successively changed to A_1 and B_1, A_2 and B_2, and so on during development. Thus a succession of changes occurs so that the contribution of the original state of the organism (A) and the various environmental factors $(B \rightarrow B_n)$ cannot be separated as each depends on the state of the other at each successive stage. Figure 2b shows for comparison an additive model which treats genotype and environment as though they were building blocks to be placed one on top of the other.

It is important to consider the implications of these considerations for understanding the development of sex differences. With an additive model (Figure 2b) the mathematical relationships between biological and social factors are straightforward: they can only exert a summating or suppressing effect on one another. It is clear how certain misleading concepts and ideas are derived from such a model: for example, that one can refer to the separate influence of genetic and environmental factors, that one can ignore one and consider only the other, that there are limits imposed on characters by genetic factors, and that culture merely amplifies or attenuates what is already there.

In contrast, such misleading concepts and conclusions would not be derived from an interactionist model (Figure 2a). Here we have, instead of simple addition or subtraction, the possibility of a variety of different mathematical relationships between the interacting influences. Some of these may be expressed easily in words whereas others would require detailed mathematical notation.

One of the most simple forms of interaction involves suppression of one influence by the other, and a number of examples of this are found in the literature on sex hormones and behaviour. A well-known example from research in animal behaviour is that of 'social inertia' in chickens described by A. M. Guhl. Typically, testosterone treatment of males induces an increase in aggression when the bird is matched with a stranger but this increase is not observed in the chicken's usual social setting where it is assumed to be overriden by habits developed in relation to the peck order.

Other types of relatively simple interactions include the

facilitation of one influence by a second which acting in isolation would have been without effect on behaviour. Research on animal behaviour again provides an example. A. R. Lumia and his co-workers either injected pigeons lowest in the dominance hierarchy with testosterone, or conditioned them to peck more dominant birds, or gave them a combination of both treatments. Male hormone alone was insufficient to increase aggression (compare with 'social inertia' described above) but aggression could be increased by conditioning. However, a much greater increase in aggression was observed in pigeons given hormones and conditioning. The extent of this increase could not have been predicted from knowledge of the simple treatment effects.

Interaction between biological and environmental factors

These examples describe the interaction of two relatively straightforward and circumscribed variables over a short period of time: to illustrate such simple principles, we relied on laboratory studies of hormonal influences in animals. When considering the continuous interaction between biological and environmental factors occurring throughout human development, such simple models as suppression and facilitation are rarely adequate. In these cases we may be not only unable to predict the extent of the outcome of the interaction, but also unable to predict its direction. Thus many studies of psychological sex differences in human development reveal correlations with opposite signs for the sexes; that is, more maternal protection producing higher IQs in girls but less maternal protection yielding higher IQs in boys. Similar effects have been found for IQ and childhood anxiety and dependency. The processes involved in such interactions cannot readily be understood on the basis of either biological sex or degree of maternal protection, anxiety, or dependence alone, but only by the interaction of both in development. To achieve such an understanding, we have to extend our view of interaction which starts from a statistical approach, involving the mathematical relationship between two isolated variables, and move to a fuller consideration of continuing development.

Julia Sherman has suggested that a combination of slower general development, later development of talking and more powerful musculature in boys, interact with the parental responses to these characteristics and produce adult sex differences in spatial and linguistic skills whose origins are to be understood only by considering the combination of influences, any one being insufficient in itself.

In a similar vein, Nicholas Blurton-Jones and M.G. Konner, in their discussion of sex differences in the behaviour of London and Bushman children, point out that the initial tendency for boys to cry more than girls may interact with the mother's response to the crying in a way which amplifies and extends the original sex differences, producing more far-reaching consequences for other forms of behaviour. Thus later behavioural differences may result whose forms could not be predicted readily on the basis of knowledge of only one or the other of the original factors involved.

These two examples suggest possible ways in which biological and cultural factors could interact over a period of time during development to produce sex differences, the source of which could not be characterised in terms of its 'inherited' or 'learnt' components, nor could it be considered as being determined by one or other of these components.

Rarely do we have the opportunity to study an entire developmental sequence so that the interplay of the many different sources of biological and environmental influences can be fully observed in context. The scarcity of such studies makes John Money's reports of his clinical experiences at the psychohormonal research unit at Johns Hopkins Hospital all the more important and illuminating.

One of the most dramatic cases involved one of a pair of male identical twins whose penis was accidentally removed during circumcision in his seventh month. Ten months after the accident the parents decided with medical advice to reassign the child's sex, and gave him a female name, clothing and hair style. When the child was 21 months old surgery was begun at Johns Hopkins Hospital to construct female genitalia. Further plastic surgery would be necessary as well as hormone replacement therapy as the child reached maturity. The child has been brought back to Hopkins for six annual visits during which her progress has been assessed and her parents given counselling. The child's mother is very sensitive to the different needs of her son and daughter and Money's account contains colourful anecdotal material of sex differences in child training practices. Although generally feminine in her behaviour, the girl's boyish traits include abundant physical energy and high activity levels but her mother tries to shape these in directions appropriate to a girl. This case is very unusual but is useful in suggesting the complexity of the processes which do eventually produce the clear differentiation of the sexes which has tempted theorists to overemphasise either the biological or the social-learning factors.

From this discussion it follows that a developmental approach is necessary to allow adequate study of the more complex forms of interaction which determine adult sex differences. Such an approach must be truly interactive rather than leaning towards either reliance on the expression of innate dispositions or the effects of social learning. A two-way process is involved which can be explained neither by socialisation acting upon the child nor by the innate expression of the child's nature regardless of the environmental consequences.

DEVELOPMENT OF THE BRAIN

Psychological studies of human development have to be set against a background of the physical maturation of the brain. This section looks at the influence of nutrition on brain development and examines the effects of specific environmental stimulation on brain cell function.

Nutrition and brain growth
ROGER LEWIN

The human brain is staggeringly complex, both structurally
and functionally, and the number of external influences that
combine to shape the personality, social colour, and intellectual potential in any individual is so large as almost to defy
analysis. But there is one factor that has been seriously under-
played in the human equation, and that is the effect of nutrition
on brain development. This situation arose because until
very recently biologists believed that the major proportion of
brain growth was complete soon after birth. But this turns out
to be a gross underestimate. It seems that at least eighty per cent
of human brain development is postnatal and occurs within the
first two years of life. This discovery, made by John Dobbing
and Jean Sands at the University of Manchester, England, has
crucial practical implications and adds an important dimension to our view of human developmental psychology.

Dobbing and Sands arrived at their picture of human brain
development by examining a number of parameters—cell
number, cell type, size, and chemical composition—in 139
human brains ranging in age between ten weeks of gestation
and seven years after birth; they also looked at nine adult
brains. The stages of development they examined followed
the widely accepted pattern. What was new in their analysis
was the *timing* of these stages.

Phases in brain growth
The first major event in brain growth—in gross terms—is the
establishment of the adult number of neurones (nerve cells).
This is followed by both an increase in the size of these cells,
and a proliferation of another population of brain cells, the
glial cells. In many respects, the function of glial cells remains
somewhat mysterious—they are said to be important for maintaining the 'health' of the neurones, and may aid in neuronal

interaction. One known role of certain of the glial cells—the oligodendroglia—is to form an insulation sheath round the axons, the long fibres extending out of neurones. This sheath, made of myelin, is crucial to the rapid electrical activity of neurones.

The brains of all species go through what is termed a 'growth spurt'—simply, when the brain is growing fastest. Typically, the brain growth spurt encompasses the multiplication of glia (of which there are eight times as many as there are neurones) and the process of myelination. Dobbing and Sands found that the adult *number* of neurones in the human brain is established by about eighteen weeks of gestation, the process having started at about week ten. Incidentally, this statement is probably supported by the timing of observed gross central nervous system malformations that occurred following the Hiroshima and Nagasaki atomic bombs—babies born with such conditions were mostly between the ten to eighteen week stage of gestation when irradiated by the bombs.

The growth spurt period of the human brain begins at about the twentieth week of gestation and is truly under way at week thirty. In their analyses, Dobbing and Sands found that the *rapid* phase of cell multiplication continues to about two years postnatal, with myelination carrying on until at least four years (see Figure 1).

Vulnerability of brain growth

There are two important points to emerge from this view of brain development, and they both concern the *vulnerability* of the brain during its growth. First, until the Dobbing and Sands report, people believed that maternal malnutrition during the last three months of pregnancy might affect the number of neurones in the infant. This is now seen to be untrue, because by that time the adult complement of nerve cells is already present. Indeed, the time at which the neurones are proliferating (ten to eighteen weeks of gestation) is too early for any maternal malnutrition to affect the process. Any brain cell deficit in an infant born to a malnourished mother is

therefore confined almost totally to glial cells. The now out-
dated view derived from the correct observation that in the
rat neuronal multiplication does take place in the nutritionally
vulnerable last period of pregnancy.

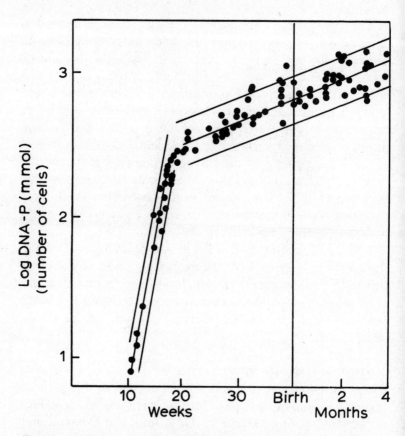

*Figure 1   A plot of cell multiplication showing the two phases of
growth: neuronal multiplication followed by glial cell proliferation.*

The second point concerns the period of nutritional vulnerability of the brain after birth. Previously, the generally held
view was that the human brain growth spurt was more or less
complete by six months, so that it should not be susceptible
to nutritional insult after that. Again untrue. The human

brain, if extrapolation from rats is correctly made, must be vulnerable to the effects of poor nutrition for at least two years after birth.

Although most of the brain follows this pattern, the cerebellum is slightly deviant. (At least one of the functions of the cerebellum is to aid in limb coordination.) It begins its growth after the rest of the brain, but finishes sooner and must therefore grow faster (see Figures 2 and 3). This means that mal-

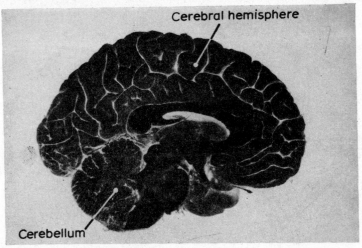

Figure 2 A medial section of the human brain showing the cerebellum and the cerebral hemisphere.

nutrition during the last part of pregnancy can reduce the number of neurones (the type known as granular cells) in the adult cerebellum. The same is true of a *few* layers in certain parts of the cerebral cortex.

Dobbing readily admits that the parameters he has measured have been those things most easily accessible to examination. He also says that almost certainly the most important part of brain development during the two years post-natal concerns the extensive production of inter-neurone connections (the axon terminals and dendrites, see Figures 4 and 5). At the moment there is no reliable way of quantifying these structures in a large number of specimens. This is a serious disability,

particularly when it comes to examining the physical consequences of malnutrition during the vulnerable period.

The consequences of early malnutrition fall into two categories: physical and behavioural. Compared with the problem
in humans, measuring physical damage in animals' brains is

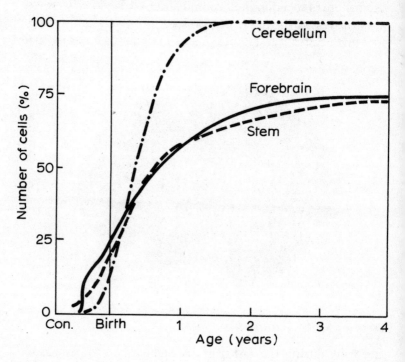

*Figure 3   A plot of growth rates showing the shorter, faster period
for the cerebellum.*

relatively easy, given the scope of current techniques. But
when it comes to examining behavioural effects, the problems
are magnified both in animals and humans. Nevertheless,
there are interesting and helpful pointers in both these
categories.

Physical aspects of brain development

The apparent uniformity of overall physical brain development
in higher animals means that one is justified in extrapolating

from experimental animals to man. The main differences are the complexity of the final product, and, more important from an experimental point of view, the timing of the stages. For instance, in terms of brain development, a newborn rat, rabbit or mouse is equivalent to a mid-pregnancy human fetus; by contrast, a newborn guinea pig compares with a two- to three-year-old human infant.

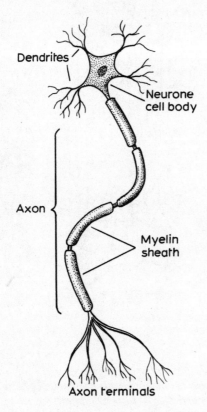

Figure 4 A diagram of a typical neurone showing dendrites, axon, and axon terminals.

The physical effects of malnutrition during the 'human' vulnerable period (the last third of gestation and the first two years post-natal) are as follows. First, the brain size is reduced to an extent that represents a true microcephaly. Second, the cerebellum suffers more than the rest of the brain in size reduction, presumably because it is growing fastest of all during the vulnerable period. Third, the number of cells in the brain is reduced, and although this is mainly confined to glial cells,

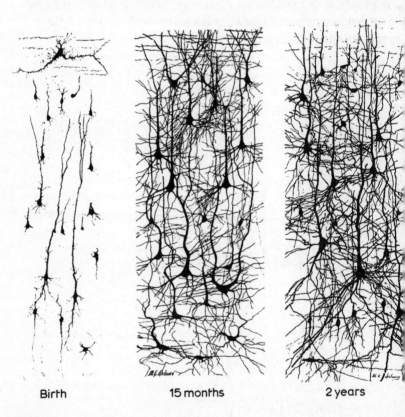

Birth 15 months 2 years

Figure 5 Photographs of sections (magnified) of the human cort *showing the increase in inter-neurone connections between birth and tv* *years of age (provided by Dr John Dobbing).*

some neurones in the cerebellum and in a few layers in the cerebral cortex are missing. Fourth, there is less lipid present, and this represents a reduced myelination of the axons. Fifth, enzyme levels are disturbed, including acetylcholinesterase, the enzyme that 'mops up' a major neurotransmitter (acetylcholine). So far, no one has been able to explain how these changes relate to malnutrition. The last physical effect, the fall in inter-neurone connections, is almost certainly the most crucial. It is unfortunate that as yet there is only one major report on it, in 1972.

It was Bernard Cragg at Monash University, Australia, who performed the almost heroic investigation on inter-neurone connections. He starved groups of rats for the first three to seven weeks of life, by which time the body weight was about one third normal. Because of the phenomenon of 'brain sparing', the brain had suffered only a twenty-three per cent weight reduction. Cragg looked at two areas of the cerebral cortex and tried to count the number of axon terminals; these are the tiny fibres that make contact with the cell bodies of other neurones (Figure 4). He found a reduction of about forty per cent in the number of terminals associated with one neurone. Cragg also suspects that some of the intact terminals are inoperative because of molecular modifications. There was no change in the number of axons, as one might have predicted because they are an integral part of the neurone itself.

Compared with the deficit in glial cells and myelination, a loss of nearly half of the inter-neurone connections is likely to be so much more important in terms of possible functional consequences. Imagine a telephone exchange with every other plug removed! The figure of forty per cent must, however, be taken as a qualitative indicator rather than a quantitative answer, for a number of reasons. First, the real difficulty in counting axon terminals reliably makes any estimate suspect. Second, almost certainly there are other factors involved, such as the amount of stimulation to which the animals were exposed. Nevertheless, a nutritionally-induced deficit of twenty per cent, or even ten per cent, in the connections between neurones would very probably affect brain function to some extent.

There are two general points about these experimental observations. All the physical effects were generated by growth restrictions that are within the 'normal' range of growth. In other words, the malnutrition was not so severe as to be unrealistic in human terms. And none of the damage was reparable by nutritional rehabilitation after the end of the vulnerable period.

Behavioural aspects

The most important facet of malnutrition in human terms is modification of behaviour. Here, animal experiments are less help, but because they represent perhaps the closest one is ever going to approach to doing controlled investigations on the problem, they are worth examining. So far there is some evidence of the behavioural consequences of malnutrition in man, some of which derives from scientific observations and some of which is anecdotal. For instance, there are indications of intellectual deficit, clumsiness, and impaired social interactions in children who are malnourished during the first two years of life. To start with, we shall look at data from animal investigations that impinge on the human situation.

First, clumsiness. The particular vulnerability of the cerebellum to nutritional insult suggests that manual coordination might be impaired by malnutrition. And this is borne out by results on rats yet to be published by Dobbing and his colleagues in Manchester. In two laboratory tests, which involved animals either running backwards on a revolving drum or crossing a chasm by means of a ladder or two parallel rods to reach food on the opposite side, undernourished rats fell or stumbled much more than control animals. While accepting the possibility of a number of other explanations, Dobbing and his colleagues postulate that 'these differences indicate impaired cerebellar function in the previously undernourished animals'. They further suggest that 'growth restriction during the human brain growth spurt on the physical growth of the cerebellum may play some part in the aetiology of clumsiness and other motor disorders of unknown aetiology.'

One now commonly agreed aspect of the behaviour of animals malnourished in infancy is a heightened excitability, a lowered threshold to external stimuli. For example, growth-retarded rats press a lever to postpone an electric shock at a higher rate than do well nourished controls, and they are more inhibited after hearing a loud noise or experiencing a shock. And in general activity experiments, undernourished rats that have been nutritionally rehabilitated move about more than normal in a free environment. (Dobbing suggests that there is at least a 'passing resemblance' between this rat behaviour and the hyperkinetic behaviour of some children.) Whether this behaviour derives from a deep psychological drive for food as a result of early deprivation (which seems unlikely) or reflects simply a higher electrical excitability of the nerve cells themselves because of lack of myelination or absence of glial cells remains mere speculation at the moment.

The Manchester team is about to publish some results on this topic that might have implications for human post-malnutrition behaviour. With Terence Whatson and Jim Smart, Dobbing observed the behaviour of previously undernourished rats in a number of social situations. It turned out that, as a general feature, the experimental animals took a more active and aggressive role in encounters between well fed and malnourished partners. Whether the social difficulties experienced by malnourished children stem from a similar effect remains to be determined.

One problem with experimental malnutrition of animals is an inevitable interference with mother/infant interactions, either by restricting food to the mother, by giving her an unusually large litter, or by preventing the normal access to her offspring. The quality of maternal care almost certainly suffers, and this could affect the later social behaviour of the young. This is a problem because it means that researchers are examining more than one variable, but at the same time it probably parallels the human situation too where social stress is closely linked with malnutrition. The observations on experimental animals are therefore certainly not invalid.

Malnutrition and environmental stimulation

The area of behavioural effects that perhaps generates most concern, but in which animal experiments are least useful, is intellectual development. Anecdotally there is a lot of evidence for impaired intellect in malnourished children, and this is backed up by a number of scientific investigations too. There have been two major surveys, one by Joaquim Cravioto and Elsie R. DeLicardie on children in Mexico, and the other by a group of researchers on Jamaican infants. A common feature between these two was the realisation of an important interaction between malnutrition and poor environment in determining overall development. Malnourished children typically come from homes that also provide a poor environmental background, and the combined deprivation appears to act synergistically.

In the Mexican study, for instance, the Caldwell Inventory of Home Stimulation—a measure of frequency and stability of adult contacts, vocal stimulation, gratification of needs, avoidance of restrictions, breadth of experience, aspects of physical environments, and availability of play materials—showed that homes that produced malnourished infants scored lower than controls. The same study revealed that children who recovered from severe malnutrition lagged behind in language ability and other aspects of intellectual development. The deficit could not be accounted for in terms of poor environment alone—malnutrition also played a part.

The Jamaican study, which was rather more extensive, was carried out by Margaret Hertzig, Herbert Birch, Stephen Richardson and Jack Tizard. It involved internal comparison of IQ performance in 74 boys aged between seven and eleven who had suffered malnutrition at an early age. The researchers also compared scores of children coming from high and low stimulation homes, giving four group comparisons. On the scale they used, well nourished children from high-stimulation homes scored 71.4 compared with 60.5 from low-stimulation environments. The scores for malnourished (but recovered) children were 62.7 and 52.9 respectively. The result shows the combined effect of under-nutrition and lack of stimulation. Tizard and his colleagues also found that the previously malnourished children were less popular than average among their class mates (as judged by subjective estimates). Dobbing describes this discovery as 'scientifically messy, but socially very important'. One is tempted to invoke Dobbing's results on the socially disturbed rats as a possible animal model of the human situation.

Although it is difficult to measure intellectual performance in animals, an effect of the combined deficit finds a good parallel in exploratory behaviour in rats. Slavka Frankova, of the Institute of Human Nutrition in Prague, has suggested a possible link between nutritional and environmental deprivation. Frankova and her colleagues have examined exploratory behaviour in rats as a test of normal behaviour. She says that 'As a uniform consequence of all forms of early nutritional deficiencies we find a lasting decrease in exploratory activity which persists for a long time after rehabilitation with a well balanced diet.' In 1970 she found that, when combined with environmental poverty as well, the diminution in exploratory activity is exacerbated. For instance, animals that suffer the combined insult show only ten per cent of exploratory activity of normals. Rats that were either malnourished or environmentally deprived showed a deficit of about thirty per cent.

More recently, in 1972, two New York researchers, David Levitsky and Richard Barnes, obtained qualitatively the same result. In their report, Levitsky and Barnes suggest two possible mechanisms through which malnutrition and environment may interact. First, the neurological effects of malnutrition may affect 'the experience or the perception of the environment . . . rendering the animal less capable of receiving or integrating, or both, the information about the environment'. Alternatively, the effect may simply be behavioural, they suggest. 'Malnutrition may produce behaviour that is incompatible with the incorporation of environmental information necessary for optimum cognitive growth . . . . the behaviour may be primarily food-oriented and, in the case of the malnourished child, the behaviour may be expressed as apathy and social withdrawal.'

In any event, when one considers the reduction in inter-neurone connections that has been demonstrated by many research groups in animals deprived of environmental stimulation, and combines that with the same effect shown by Cragg in his malnutrition experiments, a degree of behavioural disturbance is certainly to be expected.

It is therefore clear that nutritional insult on the brain during its vulnerable period damages normal behavioural development, the result presumably of the physical changes observed in the brain. At the very least, intelligence, language, motor skills, and social interactions are impaired. Closer examination of severely malnourished children, and the more difficult to identify borderline cases, will almost certainly bring to light other disabilities. As Dobbing says, 'If what we had learned from all this expensive research was that we need to feed children we would not have got very far; we all know that. The important point is that we now know the time at which the brain is most susceptible to malnutrition.' This means that countries facing nutritional problems, either chronic or acute, should make a positive discrimination in food supplies in favour of the under-twos. If this is not done the infants' brains may fail to reach their full potential and there will never be another chance to make up for it.

Brain development and the environment
ROGER LEWIN

At birth, an infant's brain contains the adult number of nerve cells, but lacks the elaborate pattern of interconnections between them that characterises the mature brain (see Lewin Chapter 17). In the adult brain there are about a hundred thousand million nerve cells, each of which carries an average of 10,000 contacts from other cells. One major problem of human (and animal) development is knowing to what extent the functional connections between nerve cells are established following a stereotyped blueprint, and how much of the organisation depends on neonatal experience.

This is not a question that can be answered by scientific study of humans, for obvious reasons. Evidence from animal experiments can, however, tell us a lot about what might happen in the human brain. During the past decade, neurobiologists in Britain and America have been examining the effect of early environmental influences on the development of vision in cats. The results have turned out to be even more remarkable than anyone could have imagined, and they have implications for our understanding of the development of the human brain, implications that concern phenomena such as learning and memory, language acquisition, visual perception, and many aspects of education.

Animals low down the evolutionary scale arrive in the world with their behavioural repertoire apparently complete. They slip into a stereotyped life with no requirement for learning about the world around them: bees know what to do with flowers, and birds can navigate over vast distances, all by following in-built rules. The higher up the evolutionary scale an animal finds itself, the more it appears to have to learn about its environment, and the more it *can* learn. And at the top (with the usual arrogance of homo sapiens) we have man, who spends many months after birth as a mewling, puking, helpless infant with scores of tasks before him to be mastered: walking, manual skills, language, thinking—the list is endless. The point of all this is that, with a brain as complex as man's, it is perhaps too much to ask that genes be able to carry all the information for weaving the final pattern of our brains. The environment therefore plays its part in shaping the finished product. One suspects that, inevitably, the finished product will reflect the environment that helped create it.

Early ideas on environmental influence

The debate about the relative contributions of genes and environment (nature and nurture) in forming the human brain goes back a very long way. Aristotle saw the brain as a kind of mental wax which recorded experience as impressed pictures. Later, metaphysical philosophers claimed that we are born into the world with some innate knowledge of it. To back their case the metaphysicians adduced the practice of geometry where new facts could be discovered not by experiments but simply by mental juggling with symbols. The nature/nurture philosophical debate was at its height in the seventeenth and eighteenth centuries when people like John Locke, William Molyneux, and George Berkeley pondered the problem.

These three philosophers considered what a man might perceive if, after life-long blindness, he was given his sight back. In other words, they were supposing that the man would 'see with infants' eyes', but be able to report with an adult mind what he saw. Locke, Molyneux, and Berkeley believed that, in order to perceive the world, the eyes (and the brain) must first experience it. Nurture, they thought, is important. If the recent experiments on cats can be extrapolated to man, these men turn out to have been correct.

The idea of 'seeing through an infant's eyes' has been followed up by a number of people. By now there are more than sixty recorded observations of people with restored sight, the first going back to the year A.D 1020. One feature is common to most of these cases—disappointment with what the visual world has to offer after a lifetime of tactile perception. Many of them become deeply depressed, and often prefer to live without lights even though some can see quite well. The two most recent cases—one examined by Richard Gregory, now at Bristol University, and the other by Carol Ackroyd and Elizabeth Warrington (both at the National Hospital, London) and Nick Humphrey (Cambridge)—yielded very different results in terms of the degree of vision restored.

Gregory's subject, S.B., had his sight restored by a corneal graft at the age of fifty-two. He was excited at the prospect of seeing what he believed to be an exciting world, but, like so many of the others, he was disappointed. His sight developed well and he learned to draw and read large writing; his distance perception was sometimes unreliable, and with new objects he preferred to use his hands in initial exploration. Although the outcome looked encouraging he soon became depressed and often chose to ignore his new channel of perception.

The second case, a girl who received a corneal graft at the age of twenty-seven, fared much less well visually. Although the image-forming powers of the eye recovered, her vision never improved beyond being able to detect large conspicuous objects, and light and dark changes. All these cases suffer from the drawback of the uncertainty about when vision failed in childhood—most of them were cases of progressive infantile corneal and lens opacity. They give the impression, though, that the adult visual system has suffered from neglect and fails to offer a true picture of what an infant sees. The fact that functional deterioration occurs, implies that the relevant nerve fibres are not permanent entities and that experience is important.

Experimental research on cats

We can now turn to the cat research which has been probing these questions by looking inside the visual cortex of animals to detect what actual physical modifications are induced by different forms of visual experience. These experiments are almost certainly relevant to the mechanisms behind other forms of adaptive experience.

The neurobiologists who started examining the cat's visual system were following a tradition of research on amphibians that appeared to imply that the wiring of the visual system was predetermined and inflexible. Ten years of investigations on cats proved this notion to be wrong, at least for those animals. The results on cats forced a re-examination of the amphibian work, and, there too, people now realise that there is much more flexibility than was once thought.

It was the two famous Harvard neurobiologists David Hubel and Torsten Wiesel who really set the research on cats on its way. In the early 1960s they devised systems for examining the responsiveness of nerve cells in the primary visual cortex of the experimental animals. They inserted minute electrodes near individual cells of the cortex and then determined what kind of visual stimulus projected onto the eye would excite these cortical cells. The cells turn out to be classical feature detectors, and the sort of feature to which they respond is an edge (or a line) of a specific orientation. Each cell responds to one orientation only, but every orientation throughout 360 degrees is represented in the complete population of cortical cells (Figure 1). Complete visual pictures are then built up in another part of the cortex by synthesising a whole set of responses to edge orientations. Hubel and Wiesel also discovered that about eighty per cent of the cells are binocular, that is they receive nerve fibres from equivalent points of *both* eyes. The remainder of the cells are connected to one eye or the other.

There is a wide range of visual feature receptors in the animal kingdom. Some are universal and are seen in almost all visual systems, while others are specific to a particular species and reflect an aspect of the animal's life-style. For instance, the frog's visual system has so-called bug-detectors which respond to small moving objects about the size of a fly— the animal's food; and flies are equipped to detect rotational movement—their companions' mode of flying. The variety of specifically responding nerve cells (whether universal or species-specific) puts enormous demands on the anatomical construction of the animals' visual systems. Can this vastly complex pattern of nerve cell wiring, especially in higher animals, be coded for in the genes, or are environmental forces required to guide the connections? It is certainly very attractive

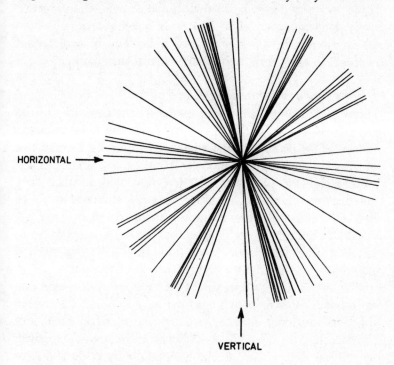

Figure 1 The distribution of optimal orientations for thirty-four cortical cells from a normal cat.

to suppose that external stimuli do play a part in the development of feature-detecting cells, especially the species-specific ones.

The visual cortex of the visually naive kitten is very different from the adult's, at least as far as feature detectors are concerned. There is still some argument among researchers about the degree of response in the young kitten, but it is clear that the cortex is at best only poorly equipped with mature feature detectors. Californian researchers John Pettigrew and Horace Barlow go so far as to say that there are no mature feature detectors in the young kitten. Hubel and Wiesel believe there is a substantial proportion (perhaps fifty per cent). And Colin Blakemore at Cambridge claims there are about fifteen per cent. He suggests that this small population is genetically determined and that it acts as a genetic organiser on which environmental stimuli can build. The binocular connections in the young animal are normal and adult.

Experiments in binocularity

Hubel and Wiesel's first experiments on the flexibility of the kitten's visual system (in 1965) concerned the stability of the binocular connections. First they tried depriving the animals of visual input totally (binocular deprivation), and then examined the binocular wiring. It had remained normal. They noted, however, that the feature-detecting ability of many of the cells was still very infantile: many of them were not orientation-selective, and some were totally unresponsive to visual stimuli. Here then was a good indication that normal experience is essential for the maturation of vision.

The result is very different if just one eye is covered and the other is allowed normal sight. Hubel and Wiesel discovered that this treatment abolishes all the binocular connections of the cortical cells. Virtually all the cells in the cortex are driven by just one eye. This time the orientation-detecting ability of the cells was normal. Hubel and Wiesel went on to find that the switch from binocularity to effective monocularity occurred after only a few days of visual exposure, as long as the exposure fell between three weeks and three months of the animal's life. During this so-called critical period there is clearly a good deal of plasticity within the visual system.

A number of other researchers have since refined this work, and they have found that the nerve connections are even more flexible than it first appeared. Blakemore and his colleagues, Rick Van Sluyters and Carol Peek have recently found that a single six-hour monocular exposure is sufficient to switch the binocular connections to the seeing eye. The switchover is not completed immediately; a period of consolidation following the exposure is required. The new monocular connections need not be permanent. If the blind eye is now allowed to see, and the seeing eye is covered, the fibres all switch over to monocularity in the other eye, within a few days. Clearly it is the active fibres from the eyes that are able to establish connections (synapses) with the cortical cells. This remarkable plasticity explains why binocular deprivation does not destroy the binocular wiring with which the animal is born: it is the *balance* of activity from the fibres that determines which ones will remain in contact with the cortical cells.

The binocular plasticity persists only until the end of the animal's critical period. Beyond that the wiring is more or less fixed. This finding has practical implications for squint (strabismus) in humans. Surgical corrections of strabismus cannot be carried out accurately until the infant is at least eighteen months old. Until the squint is repaired, the child's brain is effectively being stimulated monocularly. If the optical repair is performed after the end of a critical period for vision— supposing humans are like cats in this respect (and there is good reason to think they are)—the visual cortex will be unable to respond to adjust the connections to binocularity.

Blakemore points out that the binocular plasticity of the kitten is a good analogy—and may even be an accurate model—for learning and memory in humans. The response to the six-hour exposure followed by consolidation is similar to short-term memory followed by more permanent storage for long-term memory. By looking at the visual cortex of a monocularly deprived animal, using an electron microscope, it is possible to detect those fibres that have been active and those that have been silent. The active synapses swell up and contain more vesicles (the tiny packets that contain the chemical transmitters that pass the message from fibre to cell; Figure 2).

Plasticity of feature detectors
The results of Hubel and Wiesel's binocular deprivation experiments in the mid 1960s spurred other researchers to follow up the notion that the feature-detecting system of the visual

cortex is also plastic. By 1970 two main groups were examining the problem: Nico Spinelli and Helmut Hirsch at Stanford, and Blakemore and Graham Cooper at Cambridge. Independently, they pursued the same idea: to see if it is possible to modify the population of feature detectors by exposing the animals to an artificial visual environment—the environment consisted of vertical and horizontal stripes. Both research groups came to the same conclusion: yes, it is possible to create an artificial population of feature detectors.

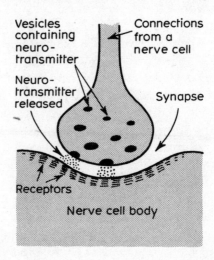

Figure 2   Diagram of a synapse between a dendrite from one nerve cell and the cell body of another.

Blakemore and Cooper kept kittens in total darkness for five and a half months, except for a few hours each day when they were placed in special enclosures that allowed them to see either vertical stripes or horizontal stripes; no animal saw both (Figure 3). At the end of the experiment the kittens were released into the real visual world to see how they fared. After a few hours adjusting to their new environment they settled down to a life in which they appeared to be virtually blind to orientations not seen during the experiment. For instance, a 'horizontal cat' would happily jump onto the seat of a chair, but would stumble into the chair legs as if it could not see them. Although the 'vertical cat' negotiated the chair legs without difficulty, it would never attempt to jump onto the seat.

Figure 3   Cat in a vertical visual world.

When Blakemore and Cooper examined the cats' brains (using the Huber and Wiesel techniques) the animals' curious behaviour was immediately explained. All the feature detectors in the horizontal cat responded only to horizontal lines, and the vertical cats had only vertical feature detectors. None of the animals had lost any cortical cells; the cells had simply been converted to one orientation-selectivity or the other; there was no in-between (Figure 4). The inevitable conclusion is that environmental input plays a large part in determining the orientation-selectivity of individual feature-detecting nerve cells in the visual cortex.

Since 1970 this conclusion has been stretched far beyond any reasonable expectation with the discovery that feature detectors can be seduced from their normal role of responding to lines, and, instead, favour tiny spots. During 1973 the California and Cambridge groups reported the effect of maintaining kittens in spotted rather than striped environments. Although some of the cells in the visual cortex did respond to particular orientations in the normal way, many of them had been converted into spot detectors—something they were simply not meant to do. Blakemore and his colleagues are now planning an ambitious series of experiments designed to discover what sort of inputs are required to create a normal cortex; they plan to explore a whole kaleidoscope of qualitatively different visual stimuli.

The degree of nerve cell plasticity in the cat's visual system is impressive, and is probably repeated in other systems in that animal and in others, including man. Of equal relevance to man, and possibly of even greater interest, is the critical period for the plasticity. Like the binocular connections, the cat's feature detectors can be modified by environmental inputs between the ages of three weeks and three months, with four to six weeks being the most sensitive period. Amazingly, Blakemore and a colleague from Dalhousie University, Donald Mitchell, discovered that just one hour exposure of a naive kitten to a visual environment at four weeks old is enough to specify the orientation-selectivity of most of the cortical cells. This result took Blakemore and Mitchell by surprise because, when they set up the experiment, they had six kittens exposed from one to thirty-three hours. This speed of nerve cell specification reinforces the analogy between learning and memory, in which irreversible changes are produced within the space of a few minutes.

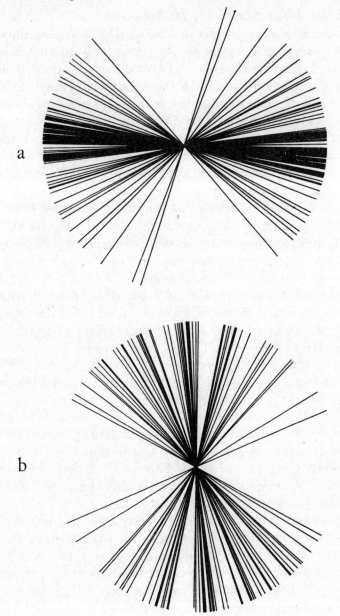

Figure 4 Preferred orientations for fifty-two cortical cells from a 'horizontal' cat (a), and for seventy-two from a 'vertical' cat (b).

Evidence for plasticity in humans

The visual sensitive period in cats starting at around three to four weeks makes good developmental sense because it is not until then that the animal's eyes are aligned accurately in their orbits, and the fluid inside the eye loses its opacity. If the visual abilities were specified before then the animal would be very poorly equipped visually to interpret its environment. What is the situation in humans? There is good evidence for plasticity in the development of the visual system. The observations on people with restored sight attest to that. And last year an intriguing experiment by two Canadians, Robert Annis and Barrie Frost, indicated that humans' vision may indeed be shaped by their visual world. For almost ten years now biologists have known that humans have a higher visual acuity in the horizontal and vertical axes than at other orientations. This may be built into the visual system, or it could result from our continual exposure to a visually rectangular world. In their recent experiment Annis and Frost examined the visual acuity of a group of Cree Indians living in tepees on the east coast of James Bay. These people had not been brought up in a rectangular urban environment.

The visual acuity of the Cree Indians was indeed different from that of the city dwellers: they had no preferred orientations for high visual acuity. The absence of orientation preference in acuity may, of course, be genetic, but it is more likely to be an environmental product. The human visual system therefore appears to be plastic, but does it have a sensitive period too? Evidence from prolonged strabismus and severe childhood astigmatism suggests that it does.

Strabismus corrected late in childhood leaves the individual with a binocular optical system, but with a visual cortex that is, to some extent at least, monocular—some of the binocular connections are lost. In his observations on severe astigmatism in infancy, Donald Mitchell finds that, later on, optical correction using spectacles fails to restore the acuity in the affected orientation. The light-sensitive cells at the back of the eye (the retina) appear to be normal. The defect is in the brain's ability to interpret the information passed to it. Adult astigmatism *can* be corrected optically.

On the evidence accumulated so far, it therefore seems fair to propose that, like cats, humans have a visual sensitive period. When is it? Without being able to adduce specific, firm evidence, one can suggest that it starts soon after birth (because humans don't have the same optical problems as cats) and continues until the age of about four years (after which astigmatism and strabismus do not leave permanent damage).

Other sensitive periods?

All this work on cats could prove to have direct relevance to development in children. For, if the visual system is equipped with a degree of plasticity to allow our brains to make note of the most likely combination of visual inputs, it is reasonable to assume similar plasticity in other brain systems, the ultimate one being learning and memory. But the question of sensitive periods is particularly important. For instance, are there sensitive periods for acquiring language, musical talent, and other congnitive activities? If so, the educational system should be shaped to exploit them.

We all acquire a degree of competence in our own language between the ages of one and four years, with no formal instruction at all. Presumably the brain is particularly receptive to acquiring language then. It therefore makes good sense to teach new languages to children nearer to the age of four years than we do at the moment. (Learning two languages at once is unwise because of interference.) The auditory system appears to be innately tuned to the human voice (see Chapter 8 by William Condon), but there is evidence that the human ear can *become* tuned to music through experience. For example, people who have acquired absolute pitch against the background of a slightly out of pitch instrument, will always be matched to that instrument's tone. And children exposed to music early in their life are known to become more musically talented than average as they grow up.

It is very important that the possibility of specific sensitive periods in infant development should be investigated. Perhaps the most crucial one is learning how to learn, how to tackle probelms. As Blakemore says, 'We don't give children problems to solve, we give them answers to remember.' If the intense innate curiosity of children in their early years is not exploited, it may be wasted for ever.

CONCLUSION

A child's life
MICHAEL RUTTER

This book has covered a variety of specific topics, mostly concerned with the period of infancy. While each chapter has had particular points to make concerning an individual piece of research or a limited aspect of development, several general conclusions keep recurring. First, it is evident that, although limited in many ways, the young infant has a surprisingly sophisticated response to his environment and quite substantial learning skills. Second, these skills and capacities have a marked influence on the process of parent-child interaction. In many instances it is the baby who shows initiative and the parent who responds by following. Third, even in the early months of life there are striking temperamental differences between infants which influence both their response to the environment and also how other people react to them. These conclusions echo those from many other investigations not reported in this book.

In addition to their theoretical implications with respect to concepts of normal development, these conclusions also have practical consequences in terms of knowledge concerning abnormalities in development. In this chapter I shall consider some of these implications. Of course, it should be said at the outset that much of the research is incomplete and many of the findings are tentative. Furthermore, the period between infancy and school age has been very little studied so that some of the crucial links in development have yet to be examined. Even so, a number of important trends are discernible.

Several of the chapters have focused on the ways in which mothers and babies respond to each other and how this process of reciprocal interaction provides the basis for developing social relationships. Genevieve Carpenter (Chapter 12) shows how young infants differentiate between the face of a stranger and that of someone they know; Aidan Macfarlane (Chapter 2) emphasises the importance of the baby's smile in encouraging his mother to give attention to him; and Colwyn Trevarthen in Chapter 7 indicates how 'conversations' play a part even in infants' early social interactions.

This, and other, research has scotched the notion that babies are mere passive recipients of adult attention. The process of interaction is both more complicated and more interesting. Several studies have shown that a high proportion of interactions are initiated by the baby and not by his parent. Furthermore, as Rudolph Schaffer (Chapter 4) argues, to a considerable extent mothers adapt and modify their behaviour in relation to their infant's patterns and cues. Infants *elicit* responses from adults and an infant's characteristics help determine how other people will respond to him. This is observable from the neonatal period onwards and has been shown by both experimental and naturalistic research. For example, Howard Moss, working at the National Institutes for Mental Health, Bethesda, found that a baby's cry serves to bring parental attention and in this way infants to some extent control parental behaviour. On the other hand, the converse also applies. Mary Ainsworth and her colleagues showed that over the course of the first year after birth, the amount and kind of attention given to babies by their mothers is strongly related to the frequency with which the infants cry during the months leading up to their first birthday. What seemed particularly important was the mother's ability to be responsive to her child's cries.

The *match* between parent and child is what matters. In this connection, individual differences with respect to both parent and child seem important. Although most parents can distinguish several different types of infant cry (hunger, pain, anger), they differ in their ability to understand infant communications and to appreciate infant needs. Infants, too, differ in what cries they give but also in the clarity of the social signals they emit. Moreover, the likelihood of a parent responding to her child's crying (or other behaviour) depends to a considerable extent on the social context in which it occurs, and the pattern of reciprocal interaction varies according to the child's level of development.

Parent-child interactions

Much has still to be learned about this developing process of parent-child interaction with respect to both its origins and its effects. But recent investigations in humans and other primates have given important leads as to what to look for, and in doing so have thrown new light on how experiences may influence behaviour. For example, Marshall Klaus and Herbert Leiderman have shown that the separation of mother and baby in the weeks after birth may have an adverse effect on mothering behaviour which lasts several months. It appears that mothering does not always 'come naturally'—it requires the stimulus of infant behaviour and the opportunity for early interaction if it is to develop optimally.

Mothering also requires adequate experiences in the parents' own childhood. Parenting is a special example of social behaviour and individuals who have been very seriously deprived of social experiences may lack parenting skills. This was shown most vividly by Harry Harlow's rhesus monkeys reared in appalling social isolation. When adult they were incompetent at mating and after eventual successful impregnation the female monkeys were cruel and rejecting parents. Of course, their upbringing was barren and empty to an extent rarely experienced by humans, but the studies were important in pointing to possible social developmental processes. Human evidence is much more fragmentary but investigations show that individuals from unhappily broken homes tend themselves to make unhappy marriages and to be less successful parents.

Animal studies have also been extremely valuable in showing the ways in which mother-infant relationships help determine how infants react to stressful experiences. This has been most elegantly demonstrated in Robert Hinde's well controlled set of investigations in Cambridge, England, in which infant rhesus monkeys were separated from their mothers for periods of one to two weeks. In his experiments at Cambridge he found that an infant's distress following separation was a function of mother-infant relationship as it existed both before and after separation. He argued convincingly that the infant's post-separation distress was not primarily due to the separation as such but rather to the consequent disturbance in maternal behaviour. Where separation leads to distortions in the mother's interaction with the infant, the infant suffers. Where separation does *not* affect the mother's behaviour, the distress in the infant is very much less.

These results with infant monkeys are paralleled by James and Joyce Robertson's carefully filmed observations of human infants during and after acute separation experiences. Early studies which showed the severe distress experienced by many toddlers following admission to hospital led John Bowlby to conclude that this was the usual response to separation and that it took the form of a kind of grief reaction. The Robertsons' recent work at the Tavistock Institute in London has cast serious doubt on Bowlby's conclusion. They found that todd-lers who were well looked after by two substitute parents in an ordinary family setting during acute separation experiences did *not* exhibit the severe distress, despair and detachment found in children admitted to hospital or to a residential nursery. The act of separation from parents carried with it certain stresses but the real damage was done by the lack of continuous personal interaction with a familiar person. When this was provided during separation, infants' responses were quite different. These findings in relation to stress experiences are very much in line with those from studies of early normal development in emphasising both the reciprocal nature of parent-infant interaction and also the importance of viewing the interaction as part of a developing process with different features at different phases of development. Investigations of the normal and of the abnormal point to the necessity to examine the content and course of parent-child interaction over time. Crude considera-tions of development in terms of children from 'broken' and 'unbroken' homes are no longer adequate.

The same consideration applies to the long-term effects of

'maternal deprivation'. Investigations in developmental psychology have demonstrated the many different facets of parenting behaviour. Parenting means providing emotional bonds or relationships, making available models of behaviour and attitudes, giving discipline and shaping behaviour, providing life experiences, and making available a network of communication. It has become apparent that the term 'maternal deprivation' covers a wide range of different experiences with quite different effects on development. Past preoccupations with parent-child separations as *the* main cause of problems now seem mistaken. Separations may be unhappy and stressful or they may be constructive and beneficial in their effects. What is more important is the pattern of family life before, during and after the separation. Again, there has to be a return to the process of parent-child interaction.

Environmental stimulation

It used to be thought that delinquency stemmed from separation experiences and 'broken homes'. Our own work and that of other investigators, especially Michael Power (London) and Donald West (Cambridge, England), has indicated that this is not so. Delinquency stems from many sources but, in so far as family experience plays a part, it is family discord and disharmony that does the damage rather than separations as such. In contrast, mental retardation and language impairment, which have also been attributed to 'maternal deprivation', can be related to a lack of the necessary linguistic and other experiences. The old concept of 'stimulation' has proved to be a somewhat misleading oversimplification. Of course, children need to be stimulated, but it is not so much the *amount* of stimulation which counts as the *meaning* of the experiences. As the studies of normal infants have shown, babies are not passive recipients of incoming stimuli and it is active social interchanges which constitute the most useful 'stimuli'.

However, these interchanges need not take place in a family setting and in this respect Bowlby's views on the inevitably bad effects of an institutional upbringing need revision. The systematic studies by Jack and Barbara Tizard at the Institute of Education, London, have shown that institutions are quite diverse and that their effects on development may be benign or malignant. It is most difficult to provide adequate care in an institution for children under two years of age, but the Tizards' work clearly shows that it is quite possible for institutions to provide the kind of experiences needed for normal intellectual and language development. However, institutions differ in the extent to which the necessary experiences are provided and they were able to show that differences in the institutional environment were systematically related to differences in the children's intellectual attainments. But, again emphasising the diversity of processes included under 'maternal depriva- tion', the Tizards found that whereas the institutional children did not differ from children reared in their own families with respect to language and intelligence, they did differ in terms of social behaviour. We are still only just beginning to disen- tangle the many threads of parent-child interaction but an important start has been made.

In this connection, it is necessary to return to the findings on individual differences between children both in infancy and later life. Most of the global theories of child development have been concerned with universals, the things that happen to all children. Thus, psychoanalytic theories discuss matura- tion in terms of stages of psychosexual development, abnor- malities being seen in terms of children becoming fixed at particular points or regressing to more primitive stages in the developmental process. Similarly, Jean Piaget discusses psychological growth in terms of stages of cognitive compe- tence, so that the child moves from the period of sensori-motor intelligence, through the stage of concrete operations to the period of formal operations (or logical thinking). Much the same applies to theories which see development in terms of biological maturation, although interestingly as long ago as 1937, Arnold Gesell, the foremost proponent of a maturational view, wrote a paper noting the importance of fundamental traits of individuality which were already evident in infancy. Recent work has shown how right he was.

Temperamental differences between children have now been

demonstrated for a wide range of characteristics both physiological and behavioural. Thus, New York researchers Wagner Bridger and Beverly Birns found consistent individual differences in the way heart rates changed in response to babies being touched and in the infants' responses to various attempts at pacifying following stress stimuli. Other workers have shown differences in mouthing behaviour, in patterns of startle response, and in conditioning. Alexander Thomas and his colleagues in New York have found substantial differences in young children's styles of behaviour with respect to characteristics such as the *regularity* of their various biological cycles (sleep/waking, hunger/satiety), their *adaptability* in response to altered circumstances, and the *intensity* of their emotional responses. Although by no means fixed, these styles of behaviour tend to remain fairly consistent over periods of several years. Other individual differences are described in the chapters by Rudolph Schaffer (Chapter 4) and Anthony Costello (Chapter 5) Corinne Hutt (Chapter 15), and John Archer and Barbara Lloyd (Chapter 16) point out that the biological differences between boys and girls have behavioural correlates which involve important consequences for psychological development.

Like most human attributes, these characteristics have a substantial hereditary component. For example, Dan Freedman showed this with respect to infants' social responses to an adult, and Anne Mari Torgersen in Norway has done the same with regard to the temperamental features included in Alexander Thomas' New York study. Of course, that is not to say that they are immutable. Other investigations have indicated that environmental influences can modify the features to an important extent.

Interest in these individual differences has focused especially on the manner in which they influence parent-child interaction and on the extent to which they are linked with later psychological problems. The importance of individual differences in temperament for later development has been shown in several rather different studies. Thus, Martin Richards and Judith Bernal in their longitudinal study of mother-infant interaction (Chapter 3) found that toddlers with sleep problems tended to be different from other children right from birth. The mothers of the sleep-problem children were in labour longer and their infants were slower to begin crying and regular breathing after they were born. In the first ten days of life the children with later sleep problems cried more, slept less and were fed more often. It is usually thought that children's sleep problems derive from parental mishandling. This study suggested that it is often the other way round, that is, the parental behaviour has been shaped by the child's sleeplessness.

Alexander Thomas' longitudinal study of middle-class families in New York found that even as early as the second year of life, and before symptoms of disorder were evident, children who later developed behavioural difficulties showed different temperamental characteristics. Children with markedly irregular patterns of functioning (as shown, for example, by the fact that they woke and went to sleep at unpredictable times), who were slow to adapt to new circumstances, whose emotional responses were usually of high intensity, and whose predominant mood was one of misery or irritability, were the children most likely to come to psychiatric notice because of behavioural difficulties some years later.

Rather similar attributes were studied by Philip Graham and his associates in a group of children of predominantly working-class London families in which one parent was under psychiatric care. The children most prone to show mental disorder a year later were those with markedly irregular sleeping, eating and bowel habits; whose behaviour lacked malleability in that it was difficult to change; and who were less fastidious, being more tolerant of mess and dirt than most children. There was also some indication that, as in the New York study, the children with disorder at home showed more negative mood and greater intensity of emotional expression.

Different temperamental attributes may put the child at risk in other circumstances. For example, Rudolph Schaffer, in a study of infants under the age of six months in a poor quality institution, found that the most active infants were those least likely to show developmental retardation in this depriving environment. Margaret Stacey and her colleagues in Swansea noted the importance of individual differences in children's response to the acute stress of admission to hospital. Children who were said to make poor relationships with adults or children who were socially inhibited, uncommunicative and aggressive, were the ones most likely to be disturbed by admission. Several studies have found that children who show restlessness, poor concentration and impulsiveness are more likely than other children to have difficulties in learning to read.

That temperamental differences are associated with the development of later problems seems clear, although the studies so far are few in number. But the main interest lies not so much in the extent of the association as in the mechanisms by which individual differences predispose or protect an individual from psychiatric disorder. These remain ill-explored as yet but several mechanisms are probably operative. In part, it is a question of individual differences in children's responses to privation and stress and in their ability to accommodate to new situations and overcome hazards. In part, temperamental attributes shape life experiences and determine children's perception of their environment and hence influence what is an *effective* environment for them. However, it seems that one of the main effects is on how other people respond to them. Thus, studies of families with a congenitally handicapped child have shown that the handicap is associated with differences in parental behaviour. Similarly, Graham found that the children with deviant temperamental characteristics elicited more parental anger than did other children. In short, individual differences (which are to some extent genetically determined) may predispose to disorder in part because they lead to the child being treated differently from other children. The distinction between nature and nurture is by no means as clear-cut as once thought. Differences in nature may lead to differences in nurture and as Colin Blakemore's work has shown (see Roger Lewin, Chapter 18) early life experiences may in turn influence brain development.

Language development

As Joanna Ryan and Richard Cromer describe (Chapters 9 and 10) it is only in the last decade or so that psychologists have become heavily involved in understanding the process of language development, and our knowledge is still very limited. Nevertheless, some of the findings already have practical implications. One of the most important discoveries has been the extent to which linguistic skills are already developing many months before the child speaks his first words. During the first twelve months of life the child's babble and pre-speech vocalisations increase in complexity and become more speech-like in their patterning. The links between babble and spoken language are still uncertain but studies by Derek Ricks and others are beginning to indicate that the patterns of babble are often abnormal in children with particularly serious disorders of language development. Much the same applies to a child's understanding of language which is well advanced some time before he is ready to speak. By careful attention to a child's use of babble, his comprehension of the spoken word and his grasp of language concepts as reflected in his play, improved diagnosis of language disorders is beginning to be possible at an earlier age than hitherto.

However, even more important have been the gains in our knowledge of how delays and distortions in the emergence of language may be associated with abnormalities in social and emotional development. It has been known for many years that children with infantile autism are almost always severely delayed in their speech development and it seemed likely that this provided a pointer to the basis of the condition. On the other hand it was difficult to see how abnormalities in speech development could cause a social defect already apparent at six to nine months when a child's first words do not usually occur until his first birthday. Resolution of this apparent paradox came from two directions. On the one hand, Beate Hermelin, Neil O'Connor, Lawrence Bartak (all in London) and others showed that it was not just speech which is impaired in autism but rather all forms of language and especially language comprehension. On the other, a variety of investigations of normal children demonstrated that language skills are already growing even in the infancy period. We do not yet know precisely which language and cognitive skills are affected in autism, but the evidence that the social disorder of autism is due in large part to a cognitive defect has important implications for treatment and especially in the use of educational methods.

Potentially, also, the knowledge deriving from studies of children's learning and perception should lead to a more rational approach to the schooling provided for normal youngsters. However, at the moment, educational applications can only be tentative and experimental. Peter Bryant's work (Chapter 14) has indicated that the Piagetian view that young children cannot grasp concepts requiring logical inferences is probably incorrect. Of course, Piaget was right in his observation that five-year-old children do not usually master such concepts but it seems that under certain circumstances they can do so. As we come to a greater understanding of the processes involved in young children's perceptions and learning we may know better how to teach them. However, that day is not yet here.

So far we have only a few of the answers we need on how children develop and why abnormalities in development occur. But compared with even a decade ago we have much improved means at our disposal to answer far more of these questions, we know better how to pose the questions, and we have a clearer delineation of the areas of ignorance that still remain.

Bibliography

Notes on the Authors

2 *The first hours, and the smile* Aidan Macfarlane

Brazelton, T.B., 'Neonatal behavioural scale', *Clinics in Developmental Medicine,* 1973, no. 50.

Darwin, Charles, 'Biographical sketch of an infant', Supplement no. 24 to *Developmental Medicine and Child Neurology,* 1971, vol. 13, no. 5.

Emde, R.N., and Harrison, R.J., 'Endogenous and exogenous smiling systems in early infancy', *Journal of Child Psychology and Psychiatry,* 1972, vol. 11, pp. 177-200.

Macfarlane, J.A., 'Olfactory factors in human attachment'. Paper to be presented at CIBA Foundation Meeting on Parent Infant Relationship, London, November, 1974.

Richards, M.P.M., and Bernal, J.F., 'Observational study of mother infant interaction', *Ethological Studies of Child Behaviour,* ed., Blurton Jones, N., Cambridge University Press, 1972.

3 *Early separation* Martin Richards

Bernal, J.F., 'Crying during the first ten days of life and maternal responses', *Developmental Medicine and Child Neurology,* 1972, vol. 14, pp. 362-372.

Bowes, W.A., Brackbill, Y., Conway, E., and Steinschneider, A., 'The effects of obstetrical medication on fetus and infant', *Monograph, Society for Research in Child Development,* 1970, vol. 35, no. 4.

Kennell, J.H., Jerauld, R., and others, 'Maternal behaviour one year after early and extended post-partum contact', *Developmental Medicine and Child Neurology,* 1974, vol. 16, pp. 172-179.

Klaus, M.H., Kennell, J.H., and others, 'Maternal attachment: the importance of the first post-partum days', *New England Journal of Medicine,* 1972, vol. 286, pp. 460-463.

Richards, M.P.M., and Bernal, J.F., 'An observational study of mother-infant interaction', *Ethological Studies of Child Behaviour,* ed., Blurton Jones, N., Cambridge University Press, 1972.

4 *Social development in infancy* Rudolph Schaffer

Aserinski, E., and Kleitman, N., 'A motility cycle in sleeping infants as manifested by ocular and gross bodily activity', *Journal of Applied Physiology,* 1955, vol. 8, pp. 11-18.

Kaye, K., and Brazelton, T.B., 'Mother-infant interaction in the organisation of sucking'. Paper given to Society for Research in Child Development, Minneapolis, 1971.

Prechtl, H.F.R., 'Problems of behavioral studies in the newborn', *Advances in the Study of Behavior,* eds., Lehman, D.S., Hinde, R.A., and Shaw, E., vol. 1, Academic Press, 1965.

Schaffer, H.R., *The Growth of Sociability,* Penguin, 1971.

5 *Are mothers stimulating?* Anthony Costello

Bayley, N., 'Consistency of maternal and child behaviours in the Berkeley Growth Study', *Vita Humana,* 1964, vol. 7, p. 73.

Costello, A.J., and Leach, P.J., 'Electronic recording of behavioral interaction'. *Determinants of Behavioral Development,* eds., Monks, F., and DeWit, J., Academic Press, 1972.

Douglas, J.W.B., Lawson, A., Cooper, J.E. and E., 'Family interaction and the activities of young children', *Journal of Child Psychology and Psychiatry,* 1968, vol. 9, p. 157.

Freedman, D.G., and Keller, B., 'Inheritance of behaviour in infants', *Science,* 1963, vol. 140, p. 196.

Mittler, P., 'Biological and social aspects of language development in twins', *Developmental Medicine and Child Neurology,* 1970, vol. 12, p. 741.

6 *The importance of play* Jerome Bruner

Bateson, G., The message 'This is play', in Herron, R.H., and Sutton-Smith, B., eds., *Child's Play,* John Wiley & Sons, 1971.

Blurton-Jones, N., 'An ethological study of some aspects of social behaviour of children in nursery school', in Morris, D., ed., *Primate Ethology,* Weidenfeld & Nicolson, 1967.

Bruner, J.S., 'The ontogenesis of speech acts', paper presented at the School of Epistemics, University of Edinburgh, 21 May 1974.

Bruner, J.S., Jolly, A., and Sylva, K., eds., *Play: its Role in Evolution and Development,* Penguin, 1975.

Hooff, J.A.R.A.M. van., 'Possible primate homologues of laughter and smiling', in Hinde, R.A., ed., *Non-Verbal Communication*, Cambridge University Press, 1972.

Miller, S.N., 'Ends, means and galumphing: some leitmotifs of play', *American Anthropologist*, 1973, vol. 75.

Piaget, J., *Play, dreams and imitation in childhood* (1946), Routledge & Kegan Paul, 1951.

Sroufe, L.A., and Wunsch, J.P., 'The development of laughter in the first year of life', *Child Development*, 1972, vol. 43, pp. 1326-44.

Weir, R., *Language in the Crib,* Mouton, 1962, The Hague.

7 *Early attempts at speech*   Colwyn Trevarthen

Ainsworth, M.D.S., Bell, S.M. and Stayton, D.J., 'Infant-mother attachment and social development', in Richards, M.P.M., ed., *The Integration of a Child into a Social World*, Cambridge University Press, 1974.

Bowlby, J., *Attachment and loss*, vol. 1, Attachment, Hogarth Press, 1969.

Guillame, P., *Imitation in Children*, University of Chicago Press, 1971.

Macmurray, J., *Persons in Relation*, Faber & Faber, 1970.

Piaget, J., *Play, Dreams and Imitation in Childhood*, Routledge & Kegan Paul, 1962.

Ryan, J., 'Early Language Development', in Richards, M.P.M., op. cit.

Schaffer, H.R., *The Growth of Sociability*, Penguin, 1971.

Wallon, H., De l'Acte à la Pensée, Flammarion, Paris, 1970.

Wolff, P., 'Observations on the early development of smiling', in Foss, B.M., ed., *Determinants of Infant Behaviour*, Methuen, 1963.

Yarbus, A.L., *Eye Movements and Vision*, Plenum, 1967.

8 *Speech makes babies move*   William Condon

Birdwhistell, R.L., *Introduction to Kinesics: an annotation system for analysis of body motion and gesture*, Washington DC, Department of State, Foreign Service Institute, 1952.

Scheflen, A.E., *Body Language and the Social Order*, Prentice-Hall, 1972.

Condon, W.S., 'Linguistic-kinesic research and dance therapy', paper presented at ADTA Convention, October 1968, published in the *Proceedings* of the conference.

Condon, W.S., 'Method of micro-analysis of sound films of behavior', *Behavior Research Methods and Instrumentation,* 1970, vol. 2 (2).

Condon, W.S., and Ogston, W.D., 'A sementation of behavior', *Journal of Psychiatric Research*, 1967, vol. 5, p. 221.

Condon, W.S. and Sander, L.W., 'Neonate movement is synchronised with adult speech: interactional participation and language acquisition', *Science,* 1974, vol. 183, p. 99.

9 The development of language   Joanna Ryan

10 Acquisition of grammar   Richard Cromer

Bellugi, U., 'Simplification in children's language', in Huxley, R. and Ingram, E., eds., *Language Acquisition: Models and Methods,* Academic Press, 1971, p. 95.

Brown, R., *Psycholinguistics,* Free Press, 1970.

Cazden, C.B., *Child Language and Education,* Holt, Rinehart & Winston, 1972.

Chomsky, N., *Aspects of the Theory of Syntax*, MIT Press, 1965.

Cromer, R.F., 'Are subnormals linguistic adults?', in O'Connor, N., ed., *Language, Cognitive Deficits, and Retardation*, Butterworth, 1975, p. 169.

Dale, P.S., *Language Development: Structure and Function*, Dryden Press, Illinois, 1972.

Ferguson, C.A. and Slobin, D., *Studies of Child Language Development*, Holt, Rinehart & Winston, 1973.

McNeill, D., *The Acquisition of Language*, Harper & Row, 1970.

Miller, G.A., and McNeill, D., 'Psycholinguistics', in Lindzey, G., and Aronson, E., eds., *The Handbook of Social Psychology*, Addison-Wesley, 1956, 2nd edition, vol. 3, p. 666.

Slobin, D.I., *Psycholinguistics*, Scott, Foresman, Illinois, 1971.

11 Competent newborns   Tom Bower

Aronson, E. and Rosenbloom, S., 'Space perception in early infancy: perception within a common auditory-visual space', *Science*, 1973, vol. 172, p. 1161

Bower, T.G.R., *Development in Infancy*, W.H. Freeman, 1974.

Bower, T.G.R., Broughton, J.M. and Moore, M.K., 'Infant responses to approaching objects: an indicator of response to distal variables', *Perception and Psychophysics*, 1970, vol. 9, p. 193.

——— 'The co-ordination of vision and touch in infancy', *Perception and Psychophysics,* 1970, vol. 8, p. 51.

12 *Mother's face and the newborn*   Genevieve Carpenter

Bower, T.G.R., 'Object perception in infants', *Perception*, 1972, vol. 1, p. 15.

Carpenter, G.C., 'Differential response to mother and stranger within the first month of life', *Bulletin of the British Psychological Society*, 1973, vol. 26, p. 138.

––––– 'Visual regard of moving and stationary faces in early infancy', *Merrill-Palmer Quarterly*, 1974, vol. 20, p. 181.

Fantz, R.L., 'Pattern vision in newborn infants', *Science*, vol. 140, p. 296, 1963.

Friedman, S., 'Habituation and recovery of visual response in the alert human newborn', *Journal of Experimental Child Psychology*, 1972, vol. 13, p. 339.

Hutt, S.J. *et al*, 'Auditory responsivity in the human neonate', *Nature*, vol. 218, p. 888, 1968.

Kagan, J., 'Do infants think?', *Scientific American*, 1972, vol. 226, (3), p. 74.

Kessen, W., Salapatek, P., and Haith, M., 'The visual response of the human newborn to linear contour', *Journal of Experimental Child Psychology*, 1972, vol. 13, p. 9.

McCall, R.B. and Nelson, W.H., 'Attention in infants as a function of magnitude of discrepancy and habituation rate', *Psychonomic Science*, 1969, vol. 17, p. 317.

Reese, H.W., and Lipsitt, L.P., *Experimental Child Psychology*, Academic Press, 1970, Chapter 2.

Salapatek, P., and Kessen, W., 'Prolonged investigation of a plane geometric triangle by the human newborn', *Journal of Experimental Child Psychology*, 1973, vol. 15, p. 22.

Schaffer, H.R., 'The onset of fear of strangers and the incongruity hypothesis', *Journal of Child Psychology and Psychiatry*, 1966, vol. 7, p. 95.

Stechler, G., 'Newborn attention as affected by medication during labour', *Science*, 1964, vol. 144, p. 315.

13 *The growth of skill*   Kevin Connolly

Bruner, J.S., 'Organisation of early skilled action', *Child Development*, 1973, vol. 44, p. 1.

Connolly, K.J., ed., *Mechanisms of Motor Skill Development*, Academic Press, 1970.

Connolly, K.J., 'Factors influencing the learning of manual skills by young children', in Hinde, R.A. and J.S., eds., *Constraints on Learning*, Academic Press, 1973.

Connolly, K.J. and Elliott, J.M., 'The evolution and ontogeny of hand function', in Blurton Jones, N., ed., *Ethological Studies of Child Behaviour*, Cambridge University Press, 1972.

——'Hierarchical structure in skill development', in Connolly, K.J. and Bruner, J.S., eds., *The Growth of Competence*, Academic Press, 1974.

15 Sex differences: biology and behaviour   Corinne Hutt

Brindley, C., Clarke, P., Hutt, C., Robinson, I., and Wethli, E., 'Sex differences in the activities and social interactions of nursery school children', in R.P. Michael and J.H. Crook, eds., *Comparative Ecology and Behaviour of Primates*, Academic Press, 1973.

Harlow, H., 'Sexual behaviour of the rhesus monkey', in F. Beach, ed., *Sex and Behaviour,* John Wiley, 1965.

Hutt, C., 'Sexual dimorphism: its significance in human development,' in F. Mönks, W. Hartup, and J. De Wit, eds., *Determinants of Behavioral Development*, Academic Press, 1972.

Hutt, C., ed., *The Biology, Psychology and Sociology of Sex Differences,* Crosby Lockwood Staples, 1975.

Hutt, C. and S.J., 'Nursery education *is* education'. *International Journal of Early Childhood* (in press).

Money, J., and Ehrhardt, A.A., *Man and Woman, Boy and Girl*, Johns Hopkins University Press, 1972.

16 Sex differences: biological and social interaction   John Archer and Barbara Lloyd.

Blurton Jones, N., and Konner, M.J., 'Sex differences in the behaviour of London and Bushman children', in *Comparative Ecology and Behaviour of Primates*, ed., Michael, R.P. and Crook, J.H., Academic Press, 1973.

Money, J., 'Biology $= \male/\female$ destiny: a woman's view', review of book, *Males and Females* by Hutt, C., *Contemporary Psychology*, 1973, vol. 18, p. 603.

Money, J. and Ehrhardt, A.A., *Man and Woman, Boy and Girl*, Johns Hopkins Press, 1973.

Sherman, J.A., 'Problems of sex differences in space perception and aspects of intellectual functioning', *Pyschological Bulletin,* 1967, vol. 74, p. 290.

17 *Nutrition and brain growth*   Roger Lewin

Dobbing, J., 'Later development of the brain and its vulnerability', in *Scientific Foundations of Paediatrics,* eds., Davies, J. and Dobbing, J., Heineman Medical Books, 1974.
Dobbing, J. and Smart, J., 'Vulnerability of developing brain and behaviour', *British Medical Bulletin,* 1974, *30,* p. 164.
Tizard, J., 'Early malnutrition, growth and mental development in man', *British Medical Bulletin,* 1974, *30,* p. 164.

18 *Brain development and the environment*   Roger Lewin

Blakemore, C., 'Development of functional connections in the mammalian visual system', *British Medical Bulletin,* 1974, *30,* p. 152.

19 *A child's life*   Michael Rutter

Richards, M.P.M., ed., *The Integration of a Child into a Social World,* Cambridge University Press, 1974.
Rutter, M., *Helping Troubled Children,* Penguin, 1975.
—— *Maternal Deprivation Reassessed,* Penguin, 1972.
—— 'The development of infantile autism', *Psychological Medicine,* 1974, pp. 147-163.
—— and Martin, J.A.M., eds., *The child with delayed speech, Clinics in Developmental Medicine,* no. 43, Heinemann Medical/SIMP, London, 1972.

Notes on the Authors

Dr John Archer is a Research Fellow in animal behaviour in the Ethology and Neurophysiology Group at the University of Sussex. His research is on the effect of sex hormones on behaviour, and sex differences in the emotional behaviour of rodents.

Dr Tom Bower is a lecturer in psychology at the University of Edinburgh. After doing research at Cornell University, New York, Dr Bower spent five years as Assistant Professor of Psychology at Harvard. Finally he moved to Edinburgh in 1969 to set up a laboratory to study infant development supported by funds from the Medical Research Council. He is the author of *Development in infancy,* published by W.H.Freeman, 1974.

Jerome Bruner is Watts Professor of Psychology at the University of Oxford. Professor Bruner, who is a self-confessed Anglophile, came to Oxford in 1972. Before that he was head of the Center for Cognitive Studies at Harvard. Professor Bruner established the Center in the early 1960s, and he has had a wide influence on the growth of developmental psychology in the last decade. The books written and edited by Professor Bruner cover a number of important areas of psychology and education. He is shortly to have published, jointly with Dr Alison Jolly, *Play: its role in evolution and development* (Penguin Press in UK).

Dr Peter Bryant is a university lecturer in psychology at Oxford. Before coming to Oxford in 1967, where he now researches on perceptual and cognitive development in children, Dr Bryant worked with subnormal children in the Medical Research Council's Social Psychiatry Research Unit in London. He has written *Perception and understanding·in young children,* published by Methuen, 1974.

Dr Genevieve Carpenter is head of the department of clinical psychology at the Belmont hospital near London and honorary senior lecturer in developmental psychology at St Mary's Hospital Medical School. Before she came to London in 1970, Dr Carpenter researched on infant perception at Boston University Medical Center, Massachusetts.

Dr William Condon is a researcher in the Division of Psychiatry at the Boston University Medical Center, Massachusetts, where he is doing work on psycholinguistics and language development in young infants, supported by the Grant Foundation.

Kevin Connolly is Professor of Psychology in the University of Sheffield. His principal research interests are in the genetics and evolution of behaviour and development in infancy and early childhood. He was awarded the Spearman Medal of the British Psychological Society in 1969 and elected a Fellow of the Society in 1971. He edited *Mechanisms of Motor Skill Development*, Academic Press 1970, and co-edited with Professor Bruner *The Growth of Competence*, Academic Press 1974.

Dr Anthony Costello is a clinical researcher in the Medical Research Council's Unit on Environmental Factors in Mental and Physical Illness at the London School of Economics where he is studying development in twins and mother-child interaction.

Dr Richard Cromer is a research psychologist at the Medical Research Council's Unit of Developmental Psychology in London where he has been studying psycholinguistics and perceptual development since 1968. Dr Cromer received his Ph.D. from Harvard University, where he spent some time with Professor Bruner at the Center for Cognitive Studies.

Dr Corinne Hutt is a senior research fellow in the department of psychology at Keele University working on exploration and play in children. Previously Dr Hutt researched in the department of psychology at Oxford on attention in early development. She has written a number of books on aspects of child development, and the latest one, *Biology, psychology and sociology of sex differences*, is to be published in 1975 by Crosby Lockwood Staples Ltd.

Dr Roger Lewin is Science Editor of the British-based international science magazine *New Scientist*. Trained as a biochemist, Dr Lewin now writes on a wide range of biological subjects and has written books on hormones, the nervous system, immunology, and learning and memory.

Dr Barbara Lloyd is a lecturer in social psychology at the University of Sussex. She is examining interactions of biological and social factors in behavioural development. With Dr John Archer, she is co-editor of a book, *Exploring sex differences,* published by Harvester Press, 1975.

Dr Aidan Macfarlane is a research officer in the department of experimental psychology at Oxford and an honorary senior registrar at the Park Hospital in Oxford. He is working on early mother/infant interactions, neonatal perception and behaviour, and ways in which psychological tests can be used in clinical medicine. Before going to Oxford, Dr Macfarlane was a teaching fellow at Harvard Medical School, where he met Professor Bruner.

Dr Martin Richards is a university lecturer in social psychology at Cambridge and does research on early infant development at the Unit for Research on the Medical Applications of Psychology in Cambridge. Dr Richards trained as a zoologist before doing research in animal behaviour, also at Cambridge. He spent two summers with Professor Bruner at the Center for Cognitive Studies in Harvard. Dr Richards edited *Integration of a child in a social world*, published in 1974 by Cambridge University Press.

Michael Rutter is Professor of Child Psychiatry at the Institute of Psychiatry, London University, where he is studying the effect of family and school influences on child development. Professor Rutter is also interested in autism and in the effect of brain damage on development. He has been visiting professor at Washington University and at the University of California, Los Angeles. His book *Maternal deprivation reassessed* was published in the UK by Penguin in 1972 and by Jason Aaronson in the US in 1975.

Dr Joanna Ryan is a lecturer in psychology at Goldsmith's College, London University. Previously she was at the Unit for Research on Medical Applications of Psychology in Cambridge, where she studied mental subnormality and language development.

Rudolph Schaffer is Professor of Psychology at the University of Strathclyde. He has been at Strathclyde for ten years studying early social development in infants. Previously he was a Principal Psychologist at the Hospital for Sick Children in Glasgow.

Dr Colwyn Trevarthen is the Reader in Psychology at the University of Edinburgh where he is studying the development of complex functions in infants. Dr Trevarthen collaborated with Dr Roger Sperry on the pioneering split-brain experiments at California Institute of Technology in the late 1950s. After working with Jerome Bruner at Harvard for two years from 1965, Dr Trevarthen went back to Caltech for a short time to study split-brain patients, and finally came to Edinburgh in 1970.